DEFENDERS OF THE FAITH
IN WORD AND DEED

FR. CHARLES P. CONNOR

DEFENDERS OF
THE FAITH
IN
WORD AND DEED

IGNATIUS PRESS   SAN FRANCISCO

Cover art: Carlo di Giovanni Braccesco
The Church Doctors: Gregory, Ambrose, Augustine, Jerome
Camera photo/Art Resource, New York

Cover design by Riz Boncan Marsella

© 2003 Ignatius Press, San Francisco
All rights reserved
ISBN 0–89870–968–7
Library of Congress Control Number 2003105178
Printed in the United States of America ∞

TO OUR HOLY FATHER, POPE JOHN PAUL II
IN THE TWENTY-FIFTH YEAR
OF HIS PONTIFICATE

His defense of the faith in our times has been unparalleled

CONTENTS

FOREWORD

When my good friend Father Charles Connor asked me to review and introduce his new book, which draws inspiration and encouragement from great figures in Catholic Church history, I was more than pleased to do so. Father Connor is an authentic teacher of history, one who makes the past come alive by writing well and at the same time drawing lessons for us from what happened in the past. His very successful series on EWTN has gone directly against our times, the prevailing view that superficially dismisses history as unimportant. Since I grew up during a previous era that some have seen as a golden age of America, from the end of World War II to the victory of civil rights, I was educated with a knowledge of and enthusiasm for history. In those days any thinking high school or college student knew the truth of the saying that those who did not study history were bound to repeat it, especially its mistakes.

It is actually amazing how quickly a working knowledge of history disappeared among young Americans and how an awareness of the fascinating history of the Catholic Church vanished from Catholic education. When I recall incidents from history to the members of my community, I am amused that our young friars think I am extraordinarily learned, but all I am actually doing is recounting what any moderately well-educated Catholic of the mid-twentieth century had been taught.

Father Connor is one of the few intrepid souls working to reverse our chronic religious, civic, and clinical amnesia. And he is all the more interesting since he is clearly not one of those historians who simply pile on the facts. Instead he teaches in order to present the broad sweep of events and their relationship to one another. Following the model of Saint Augustine's *City of God*, Father Connor, like the great Bishop, relates the significant events to the history of salvation. In history thus conceived, people do not simply perform deeds, but they react to God's unfolding Providence. Father Connor uses the very reliable method of describing people and not simply events or things. He paints portraits of important and inspiring people at significant moments in Church history, beginning with a selection of martyrs and ending with some of the most interesting people of our times like Cardinal Mindszenty, Father Walter Ciszek, and Cardinal Ratzinger.

This book will be helpful for serious students of any age, that is, people who are determined to learn for their own growth and development as human beings and Christians. While Father Connor is not presenting original research, he makes use of several primary sources and standard works that can lead the reader to more detailed accounts. Most of the great Christians we meet in this book are the subjects of serious biographies and scholarly analyses. What Father Connor does is bring to life names that may be already familiar, like Augustine and Aquinas, and some that may be less well known, like Athanasius, John Fisher, and my own dear friends Frank Sheed and Maisie Ward.

This book comes at a crucial and painful moment in Catholic Church history. The present era—one of creativity but also of dissent, of apparent development as well as confusion, of great activity but of many losing their way—is coming to end. Like most other eras, I think it will be seen as a field sown with wheat and weeds. At the beginning of the third millennium we witness an era of weakened and eroded Catholic identity. It is a time of incredible cultural mediocrity, in which many young people, despite a good deal of life experience, suffer from a seriously deficient education. This is particularly regrettable because the young obviously try and want to learn, but often they are given contrived experiences and a sadly inadequate education. A recently compiled high school text of several hundred pages about the history of the United States mentioned neither Washington nor Lincoln, because "we don't need heroes". This attitude is similar to Catholic religious education that scarcely mentions the sacraments or, God forbid, the divinity of Christ.

Defenders of the Faith—in Word and Deed is something refreshingly different. This work is part of a sea change beginning to take place now in Catholic education: history with heroes, history with passion, conviction, and heart. Here we find examples of valiant disciples of Christ who, in spite of their very bad times, remained faithful and dynamic in their response to that mysterious and unique entity that Christ established to bring his life, teaching, and sacraments to the world until the end of time.

Father Benedict J. Groeschel, C.F.R.

I

Early Christian Martyrs of the Roman Empire

In the year A.D. 111, Pliny the Younger wrote to the Emperor Trajan, informing him how the persecution of the Christians was going:

> The method I have observed toward those who have been denounced to me as Christians is this: I interrogated them whether they were Christians; if they confessed it I repeated the question twice again, adding the threat of capital punishment; if they still persevered, I ordered them to be executed.... The temples, which had been almost deserted, began now to be frequented ... and there is a general demand for sacrificial animals, which for some time past have met with few purchasers.

To which Trajan replied:

> The method you have pursued, my dear Pliny, in sifting the cases of those denounced to you as Christians is eminently proper ... *no search should be made for these people*; when they are denounced and found guilty they must be punished; but where the accused party denies that he is a Christian, and gives proof ... by adoring our gods, he shall be pardoned....

13

Information without the accuser's name subscribed must not
be admitted in evidence against anyone.[1]

Our Lord's Apostles brought the gospel message to a Roman
Empire that, in geographical terms, did not substantially differ from the one in which Constantine proclaimed Christianity the official religion in the fourth century. Octavian
Augustus is usually considered the first Roman Emperor, one
who ushered in two centuries of relative tranquility. Most
descriptive sources fix the boundaries of the Empire at Ar-
menia and Mesopotamia, the Arabian Desert, the Red Sea,
Nubia, the Sahara, the Moroccan mountain ranges, the At-
lantic Ocean, the Irish Sea, Scotland, the North Sea, the
Rhine, the Danube, the Black Sea and the Caucasus. In addition, Augustus is also credited with adding territory along
the North Sea west of the Elbe and areas in the vicinity of
the Danube.

In this vast political setting, religion was very much a personal affair. Families, and even individuals, could have their
own deities, although it was not at all uncommon to find
entire cities worshipping one god. The state tolerated this,
provided the religious cult or personal belief was not hostile
to the government or so exclusive as to appear suspect.

Judaism was a separate case. It had a certain exclusivity
about it, in that no Jew could belong to another cult nor be
allowed to participate in any type of emperor worship. One
would think Jews would be severely punished, if not persecuted. Instead, Judaism was officially protected in the Empire. The reason was curious: Jews were a part of a nation

---

[1] Pliny the Younger, Letters, Loeb Library, cited in Will Durant, *The
Story of Civilization: Caesar and Christ* (New York: Simon and Schuster, 1944),
3:111, 648.

subject to Rome. Their religion and nationality were syn-
onymous, and Judaism was not a sect likely to attract non-
Jewish adherents. Furthermore, their numbers were not
expected to increase dramatically, hence their lot was not an
unhappy one as far as being tolerated by the Empire went.

Christians would not be as fortunate. At first, the Roman
officials saw them as a sect within Judaism. There were so
many deities worshipped within the Empire that if a particular Jewish sect gave allegiance to one Jesus of Nazareth it
made slight difference. It was the Jews themselves who first
noticed all was not well within their ranks. Early followers
of Christ were moving away from the strict observance in
alarming numbers; their new faith seemed to be shaking Judaism to its foundation. In such a charged atmosphere, certain Jews were only too happy to report on Christians to the
authorities, sparking an official scrutiny. The government
agreed Christians were becoming a divisive force and were
in violation of the Roman law:

> To this legal suspicion of the Church as a religious conspir-
> acy, there was added very soon the more fruitful suspicion of
> its members as monsters of depravity, meeting secretly for
> the performance of rites, bloody and unnaturally obscene.[2]

It is true that Christians lived in a somewhat tense atmosphere for the first three centuries of the Church's life. It is
not true that persecution was unceasing; rather, it was inter-
mittent, sometimes limited to the city of Rome, sometimes
extending throughout the Empire. A popular legend evolved
through the centuries about when anti-Christian hostility
became intense, believers would hide from Roman officials

[2] Philip Hughes, *A History of the Church*, rev. ed. (New York: Sheed and
Ward, 1949), 1:158.

in the catacombs, underground burial places on the outskirts of the city. These were not secret hiding places; in fact, they were well marked on city maps. It so happened that the soft turf of the region could be easily excavated and developed into a large network of subterranean tunnels, which could be utilized for several purposes, burial among them. Christians (and, for that matter, Jews as well) found the system of underground burial ideal in a city where space was at a premium. In addition, the catacombs provided a space for gathering for the celebration of the Holy Eucharist and for Christian artists to leave for posterity a fascinating record of a vibrant faith.

This is not to minimize persecutions. They occurred with ferocity, and many martyrs and defenders of the faith came forth. They were martyrs because they died under some excruciating form of torture; they were defenders of the faith because of their witness to Christ as their only Lord, to the exclusion of all others, including the emperor. We know of their persecutions and martyrdoms from three principal sources: the accounts of non-Christian historians, the minutes of their trials (known as the Acts of the Martyrs), and eyewitness accounts.

The earliest persecutions seemed to have occurred under the Emperor Nero (54–68) and may well have been an attempt to turn the attention of Rome's citizens away from the Emperor's own burning of the city. It was a persecution limited to Rome itself, and both Peter and Paul are believed to have been victims of it. Tacitus, a Roman historian, pictures it vividly:

> First, then, the confessed members of the sect were arrested; next, on their disclosures, vast numbers were convicted, not so much on the count of arson as for hatred of the human

race. And derision accompanied their end: they were covered with wild beasts' skins and torn to death by dogs; or they were fastened on crosses, and, when daylight failed, were burned to serve as lamps by night. Nero had offered his gardens for the spectacle, and gave an exhibition in his circus, mixing with the crowd in the habit of a charioteer, or mounted on his car. Hence, in spite of a guilt which had earned the most exemplary punishment, there arose a sentiment of pity, due to the impression that they were being sacrificed not for the welfare of the state but to the ferocity of a single man.[3]

"Incest" and "cannibalism" are hardly terms to be thrown about lightly. They were, however, among the most common accusations made against Christians. Even more curious was the charge of atheism. It was assumed that since Christians did not practice the religion of the state, the worship of the pagan gods, that they had no religion. If this persisted, the gods would become angry and inflict all sorts of wrath on Roman society.

To these charges were added arguments put forth by philosophers and men in political life, trying to reason on a somewhat higher level. These men claimed that Christians concentrated their proselytizing efforts on women, children, and slaves, classes of society wont to believe anything. Further, they felt this new sect had little use for Roman ancestral customs, and the objection of some to military service was highly suspect. Arguments were made against the efficacy of Christian Baptism, the consistency of scriptural accounts, and even the Incarnation: Why would a perfect, changeless God, they wondered, ever wish to become a tiny

---

[3] Tacitus, *Annals*, bk. 15, chap. 44, cited in Jean Comby, *How to Read Church History* (New York: Crossroad, 1992), 1:38.

babe? Finally, the physical, bodily Resurrection of Christ was taken to be the most bizarre notion of all. According to Porphyry, a Hellenized Jew from Tyre who had studied under the philosopher Plotinus, the Paschal Mystery was

> a remarkable lie . . . ! If you sang that to mindless beasts which can do nothing but make a noise in response you would make them bellow and cheep with a deafening din at the idea of men of flesh flying through the air like birds, or carried on a cloud.[4]

The Christians answered, always in charity. One of the most famous responses was a description of their community written for the benefit of civil magistrates by Tertullian of Carthage. The courage of so many Christians had converted Tertullian from paganism, and he used his great writing talent to defend his newfound religion:

> We are a body knit together by the sense of one belief, united in discipline, bound together by a common hope. We form an alliance and a congregation to assail God with our prayer, like a battalion drawn up for combat. This violence God delights in. We pray, too, for the emperors, for their ministers and all in authority, for the welfare of the world, for the prevalence of peace, for the delay of final consummation. . . .
>
> But it is mainly the deeds of love so noble that lead many to put a brand of infamy on us. 'See how they love one another', they say, for they themselves are animated by mutual hatred. And they are angry with us, too, because we call one another brother; for no other reason, as I think, than because among themselves names of affinity are assumed only in a mere pretence of affection. . . .

[4] Porphyry, *Against the Christians*, cited in Comby, *How to Read Church History*, 1:33.

> We live with you, eat the same food, wear the same cloth-
> ing, have the same way of life as you; we are subject to the
> same needs of existence. We are not . . . living in woods and
> exiling [ourselves] from ordinary life. . . . We live in the same
> world as you: we go to your forum, your market, your baths,
> your shops, . . . your inns, . . . we serve as soldiers with you,
> and till the ground and engage in trade.[5]

The early second century witnessed persecutions under Trajan (98–117). Tradition tells us that Saint Clement of Rome
was martyred at this time and that Saint John the Evangelist,
the only Apostle to die a natural death, suffered an intense
passion near the Latin Gate of the city of Rome.

Trajan was succeeded some forty-four years and three emperors later by the philosopher Marcus Aurelius (161–180).
During his reign, the apologist Justin was sentenced in Rome
and Polycarp, the saintly Bishop of Smyrna in Asia Minor,
was martyred. During this period, too, we have the earliest
evidence of the presence of Christianity in Gaul—the area
of present-day France—and specifically the city of Lyon. In
177, the Christians of Lyon described in detail the martyrdoms of many of their own; in particular, they speak of Pothinus, a ninety-year-old bishop; Sanctus, a deacon; and
Blandina, a slave girl. Eusebius, one of the earliest Church
historians, noted of each martyrdom: Pothinus, with great
difficulty breathing, "conveyed to the tribunal by the soldiers, escorted by the city authorities and the whole multi-
tude, who gave utterance to all sorts of cries, as if he were
Christ himself; and so he gave the good witness." Sanctus,
the deacon's entire body bruised, was "unbending, un-
yielding, . . . for he was bedewed and strengthened by the

---

[5] Tertullian, *Apology*, chaps. 37, 39, 42, cited in Comby, *How to Read Church History*, 1:36.

heavenly fountain of the water of life which issues from the side of Christ." Blandina, the slave girl, acknowledged even by those of the hardest heart to have been tortured beyond anything ever witnessed, was "suspended on a stake, was exposed as food to wild beasts which were let loose against her".[6]

What sorts of thoughts went through the Emperor's mind as he witnessed such happenings? What emotions swelled up inside him as reports of brutal slayings reached his ears? The famous British essayist and defender of the faith G. K. Chesterson tried to put himself into the mind of Emperor Marcus Aurelius to answer these questions:

> It was not exactly what these provincials said; though of course it sounded queer enough. They seemed to be saying that God was dead and that they themselves had seen him die. This might be one of the many manias produced by the despair of the age; only they did not seem particularly despairing. They seemed quite unnaturally joyful about it, and gave the reason that the death of God had allowed them to eat him and drink his blood. According to other accounts, God was not exactly dead after all; there trailed through the bewildered imagination some sort of fantastic procession of the funeral of God at which the sun turned black, but which ended with the dead omnipotence breaking out of the tomb and rising again like the sun. But it was not the strange story to which anybody paid any particular attention; people in that world had seen queer religions enough to fill a madhouse. It was something in the tone of the madmen and their type of formation. They were a scratch company of barbarians and slaves and poor unimportant people; but their for-

[6] Eusebius, *Church History*, bk. 5, chap. 1, cited in Comby, *How to Read Church History*, 1:41.

mation was military; they moved together and were very absolute about who and what was a part of their little system; and about what they said, however mildly, there was a ring like iron.[7]

The second century gave way to the third. The stories of the martyrs continued to be filled with heroism. Felicity, a slave girl who was a companion to the noble lady Perpetua in Carthage, was martyred in 203. She was eight months pregnant when captured, and the law prohibited the execution of pregnant women. She gave birth to a little girl, who was subsequently adopted by a Christian woman. Felicity refused to sacrifice to the gods; when asked what she would do when she was handed over to the wild beasts, her response was not uncommon: "Now it is I who am suffering what I am suffering. But there another will be in me who will suffer for me, because it is for him that I shall be suffering."[8]

Some half a century later during the persecutions of Valerian, Cyprian, the Bishop of Carthage, bore witness to Christ. After his apprehension, he stated to the proconsul that his name was Thascius Cyprianus. He admitted that he was the bishop who refused to participate in any rituals honoring the Roman gods. The proconsul warned that his life was at stake and the matter was not to be taken lightly. Cyprian responded that far from taking anything lightly, the matter was so clear as not even to merit discussion. When sentence came that he was to die by the sword, he responded with a sincere "Deo Gratias."

[7] G. K. Chesterton, *The Everlasting Man* (San Francisco: Ignatius Press, 1993), 163–64.

[8] *Acts of Perpetua and Felicity*, cited in Comby, *How to Read Church History*, 1:42.

In all probability, the reign of Valerian also witnessed the martyrdom of Deacon Tarsicius. His story is well known. One day he was bringing the Holy Eucharist to a sick member of the community, guarding it very carefully. He was stopped by soldiers who demanded to investigate what he was carrying. When he refused, he was beaten to death.

In August 258, at the height of Valerian's persecutions in Rome, Pope Sixtus gathered with many of the faithful in the catacombs of Saint Callixtus (the official cemetery of the Church of Rome). Warren Carroll, in his *Founding of Christendom*, captures this devout, though undoubtedly fearful, gathering:

> Pope Sixtus was preaching. With a trampling rush, the soldiers burst into the crypt. The congregation drew together before them ... to signify that they were ready to die to defend the Pope. But Sixtus, like his Lord in Gethsemane, would have none of that. He came forward and they took him, along with four of his Deacons. ... Another Deacon, Lawrence, cried out, "Father, where are you going without your Deacon?" Sixtus replied: "I do not leave you, my son. You shall follow me in three days." The Vicar of Christ was taken up the nearby stairs to the open air and beheaded on the spot, along with the four Deacons.[9]

Lawrence did follow in three days, being roasted on a gridiron, even managing some lightheartedness by asking to be turned over because "one side is broiled enough". Lawrence is today honored by several churches in the Eternal City and fittingly enough, because it was for that very city he prayed while preparing to die. A few days later a group of Chris-

---

[9] Warren H. Carroll, *The Founding of Christendom, History of Christendom* (Front Royal, Virginia: Christendom Press, 1985), 1:497.

tians were buried under a deluge of rock and elements as they were assisting at the Holy Sacrifice of the Mass. The event took place near the tombs of Saints Chrysantius and Daria. For some centuries after the excavations of Pope Damasus I, pilgrims to Rome could view what had happened. The remains of many of the faithful of all ages, along with priests and deacons holding sacred vessels, were clearly visible. It would be difficult to picture a scene eliciting more faith.

The last of the great persecutions against Christians took place during the reign of Diocletian at the beginning of the fourth century. It extended throughout the Empire and lasted for a full decade (303–313). At the same time, Diocletian's empire was beginning to crumble. He had divided his vast realm into four divisions, with a separate emperor in charge of each. As the years progressed, four emperors gave way to seven, with periodic warfare among them. One would be victorious and defeat his rivals—Constantine, the son of a Christian mother named Helena. When he routed his chief adversary, Maxentius, at the Battle of Milvian Bridge near Rome in 312, civil war ended, freedom was accorded the Church, and, in due time, Christianity became the religion of the Empire. We know from the writings of Lactantius and Eusebius, both Christians, that Constantine's victory was attributed to the supernatural. He had seen a vision, words written in the heavens, which he would eventually incorporate on Roman coins: "In Hoc Signo Vinces"—"In This Sign You Will Conquer." In the vision, these words surrounded a cross, the symbol of Christianity, the religion Constantine would make normative.

A question long debated is the exact number of Christians martyred in the Church's first three centuries. French historian Jean Comby tries to answer:

People used to speak in terms of hundreds of thousands, even of millions, of victims. These figures are altogether exaggerated. . . . [M]odern historians tend only to count the martyrs of whose names and manner of death we have a record. This considerably reduces the numbers: less than three thousand for the last persecution. No doubt the truth lies somewhere in between these two extremes.[10]

This much is certain: those early Christian martyrs of the Roman Empire who bore witness to the Lord Jesus with their lives were the Church's earliest defenders of the faith. It was they who, in the Communion of Saints, undoubtedly prayed for the peace of Constantine, a peace well captured by Eusebius:

It was possible to see, like a light shining forth out of a dark night, churches being put together in every city, and crowded assemblies, and rites being performed at these according to custom. And every one of the unbelieving heathen was struck not a little at these things, marveling at the wonder of so great a change, and proclaiming the God of the Christians as great and alone true.[11]

---

[10] Comby, *How to Read Church History*, 1:45–46.

[11] Eusebius, *Ecclesiastical History*, bk. 9, chap. 1, cited in Carroll, *Founding of Christendom*, 513.

II

Athanasius and Augustine

When one refers to "the West" of the fourth century, one is actually speaking of the western portion of the Roman Empire, configured as it was in A.D. 379 by Emperor Gratian. It included

> the Pretorian Prefectures of Italy and the Gauls, the dioceses of Italy, Rome, Africa, Gaul, Spain and Britain, all Europe west of the Rhine, south of the Danube, and west, roughly, of the meridian of 20 deg. E. with, in Africa, the modern Morocco, Tunis and Tripoli.[1]

The Church had been given a great deal of liberty by Constantine after 313, but it almost seems a price had to be paid for such freedom. Subsequent Roman emperors thought nothing of involving themselves in ecclesiastical matters. If they felt a theological controversy warranted their intervention, such would happen. If they felt some matter of discipline or Church policy required the attention of a council, that council would become a reality.

[1] Philip Hughes, *A History of the Church*, rev. ed. (New York: Sheed and Ward, 1949; 1979), 2:1.

One would think the fourth century would have been intensely spiritual. Converts were coming to Christianity in large numbers, and the faithful were being nourished by the writings of the Desert Fathers, the holy hermits, and books on ancient monastic observance. In fact, many conversions were pure political expediency, and everyone was not quick to pick up spiritual reading. Further, the clergy was becoming secular in thought and worldly in lifestyle. The emperor had set up a Christian court in Constantinople, which gave him a freer hand in his dealings with the Pope. Unfortunately, many clergy felt much more drawn to the East, in particular, Constantinople's social milieu. Above all, the fourth century witnessed a long and difficult controversy, which had its beginnings at the time of Constantine, a controversy engaging the greatest intellects of the day. That controversy concerned Arianism.

The heresy took its name from Arius, a priest from Alexandria, Egypt. Arianism was a denial of the divinity of Christ, a system of thought that set about proving the Second Person of the Blessed Trinity to be little more than first among equals in creation. He was the greatest of creatures, perhaps, but still a creature and therefore not eternally existent with the Father. If the title "Son of God" were given Christ, it might be some designation of honor, but could not be taken literally.

The reaction to Arius was quick and divided. By 323, he had made surprising inroads among Eastern bishops, whose support would naturally filter down to the clergy and laity of their dioceses. Arius' own bishop, Alexander of Alexandria, was another matter. He demanded a clear statement of the priest's views, which he presented first to his presbyterate and later to a council composed of Egyptian bishops. Two bishops were in apparent agreement with Arius, while the overwhelming consensus declared him a heretic and ordered that he, along with eleven like-minded priests and deacons, be deposed. Arius then made his way to Caesarea, where he would be freer to teach his new doctrine. Once again, a sizeable number of Syrian bishops seemed strongly attracted to his views.

The Emperor Constantine knew full well that Arianism was dividing the Empire theologically and politically and must be settled. He therefore convoked the first ecumenical council in Church history at Nicaea, in Asia Minor in 325. The most famous definition to emerge from this council declared Jesus Christ to be *homoousios*, meaning he is consubstantial and coeternal with God the Father. Alexander of Alexandria, Arius' bishop, fought hard for the introduction of this term and succeeded in obtaining the Emperor's approval of the same. The Council of Nicaea declared formally what had always been the faith of the Church. The Church professed her faith in

> one Lord Jesus Christ, the Son of God, begotten of the Father, Only-begotten, that is, from the substance of the Father; God from God, Light from Light, Very God from Very God, begotten not made, Consubstantial with the Father, by Whom all things were made, both things in heaven and things in earth; Who for us men and for our salvation came down and was incarnate, was made man, suffered, and rose again the third day, ascended into heaven, and is coming to judge living and dead.[2]

The Council of Nicaea did not end the Arian heresy; it merely condemned it. Struggles would continue for decades between

---

[2] Stephenson, *A New Eusebius*, 366, cited in Jean Comby, *How to Read Church History* (New York: Crossroad, 1992), 1:92.

those who supported Arius' theology and those who opposed it. These struggles often turned into personal animosities. Charges and countercharges were leveled between both camps, and bishops and priests often found themselves excommunicated, if not exiled. There was one bright light, however, one great defender of Nicene orthodoxy.

When the Council of Nicaea opened, Bishop Alexander of Alexandria brought his secretary with him, a young priest named Athanasius. The Bishop had known the young man most of his life, perhaps even since the latter's childhood, when he played near the cathedral of Alexandria. Seven years as the Bishop's secretary in 325, Athanasius was already well known for a scholarly work he produced on the Incarnation. Most biographers point to his unusually fine education in legal studies, philosophy, theology, and rhetoric, one of the most esteemed areas of learning in the fourth century. Born in Alexandria about 297, he was taught by a number of priests who had witnessed firsthand and had served as confessors during the persecutions of Maximian, which were especially intense in Alexandria.

Athanasius was in his late twenties when he became Bishop of Alexandria on the death of Alexander (his mentor had nominated him for the see); once in office his tenure would prove very turbulent. He began with a tour of the vast diocese, and because of his ascetic nature, concentrated on the visitation of monasteries. He was intent on restoring unity, but his enemies were just as resolved to keep up the fight. Arianism had made great strides in Egypt and Asia Minor and had built up powerful allies. In 330, Emperor Constantine received a letter from one such figure—Eusebius, Bishop of Nicomedia. He asked the Emperor to write to Athanasius and try to persuade him to reconcile with the Holy See. Athanasius responded that the Catholic Church could "hold no communion with heretics who denied the divinity of Christ". In his view, the denial of our Lord's divinity, from whatever source it came, weakened the great importance of Christ's birth in salvation history. Once that was accepted, his redemptive death for sinful humanity became meaningless. Athanasius developed these positions and expressed them forcefully in *Discourses Against the Arians* and *The History of the Arians*.

Athanasius was less a scholar than an apologist. He was less concerned with intellectual nuances than with a spirited defense of the faith:

> In reality it must be said that as an "authentic Father of the Christian faith", as Pachomius, one of the founders of early monasticism, called him, he was not so much concerned with the conceptual development of the data of revelation as with the defense of the sound points of the doctrine he had received. He was a pastor and a man of the church rather than a theologian, and he was immersed even to the point of harsh and violent polemics in an existence which was totally a profession of faith: unpolished, overwhelming and absolute. No disaster, no temporary failure, however serious or dangerous, succeeded in stopping him or turning him aside from the course he had taken.[3]

He would pay dearly for such tenacity. In the forty-six years he served as Bishop of Alexandria, he was exiled five times, usually on the most superficially concocted charges. Estimates vary, but it may safely be said he spent seventeen to twenty years away from his see, thanks to the work of his

[3] Pier Franco Beatrice, *Introduction to the Fathers of the Church* (Vicenza, Italy: Edizioni Istituto San Gaetano, 1983; English edition 1987), 197, 199.

Arian adversaries. The last seven years of his episcopacy were somewhat peaceful. He was unchallenged in the occupation of his diocese and is believed to have written his *Life of Saint Antony*, the famous Desert Father.

How judge Athanasius? Perhaps by this measure:

> The greatest man of his age and one of the greatest religious leaders of any age, Athanasius of Alexandria rendered services to the Church the value of which can scarcely be exaggerated, for he defended the faith against almost overwhelming odds and emerged triumphant. Most aptly has he been described by Cardinal Newman as "a principal instrument after the Apostles by which the sacred truths of Christianity have been conveyed and secured to the world".[4]

Athanasius died in Alexandria on May 2, 373. He influenced many, including a young man in Africa named Augustine, who apparently had read Athanasius' writings on monasticism and took them as a guide for his own development of the monastic life. Much like Athanasius, the Bishop of Hippo would also be called upon to become a strong defender of the faith.

Augustine was born in 354 in Tagaste, an area known today as Souk-Ahras in Algeria. In his time the area was contained within the province of Numidia in North Africa, itself a province of the Roman Empire. Though his family origins were quite humble, he obtained an excellent classical education in a cosmopolitan setting.

Such training did not diminish his pride in his humble origins. We know much of Augustine, not the least of which

---

[4] Herbert Thurston, S.J., and Donald Attwater, eds., *Butler's Lives of the Saints* (Westminster, Md.: Christian Classics, 1988), 2: 216.

is his father's pagan origin and the fact that his mother, Saint Monica, was a devout Catholic who, having prayed many years for the conversion of her son, has inspired Christians of all ages to persevere in prayer.

Augustine's primary and secondary education was received near his native town. From there he went to Carthage, the largest city in Africa and second largest after Rome in the West. Fourth-century classical education demanded the study of rhetoric, the art of writing and speaking. Of all disciplines, this was the most vital for one's successful future. If pursued seriously, it could lead one to financial comfort and personal prestige.

Even more intently, Augustine studied philosophy. One essay Cicero had written on wisdom particularly fascinated him; he took it as a way to live his life, thus establishing a foundation upon which to build his later Christian thought.

Often called the Doctor of Grace, Augustine was an even more convincing defender of the faith, in light of his own journey to Christianity. For many years he lived an immoral life. In fact, his *Confessions* describes his sexual relationship with his mistress as an obsession. This relation continued for fourteen years and produced a son, Adeodatus, who would die in his eighteenth year, but not before being baptized.

The early Augustine was not only a promiscuous man; he was also devoid of faith. Religious belief was the lot of the simple, uneducated souls, he felt. A rationalist school of thought that greatly attracted him, Manicheanism, reinforced his view. The Manicheans taught that reason could explain the great mysteries of life and provide us the only sure knowledge we could have. They also maintained that the eternally opposite principles of good and evil, light and darkness, were locked in combat with each other. These were forces beyond the control of human beings. This idea was tremendously consoling to Augustine. He could continue to lead an evil life and argue in his own mind that something totally beyond him controlled his sinfulness.

The more Augustine read of Mani, the founder of the Manichean sect, the more disillusioned he became. Such disillusionment was clearly the work of the Holy Spirit. Augustine's growing perception of the arrogance found in Manicheanism was the Spirit's leading him humbly to accept the Church's magisterial role.

As a professor of rhetoric in Italy, he came under the influence of Saint Ambrose, the Bishop of Milan. Ambrose's sermons allowed Augustine to discover how different the Christian faith was from what he imagined. At the Easter Vigil in 387, Augustine and his son were both baptized, and one can still view the excavations under Milan's magnificent cathedral, where this marvelous event occurred. Augustine's life (after the death of his son) is well known; it was a life in accordance with a rule, and later the life of a priest, a bishop, and, particularly, Bishop of Hippo in Africa. As bishop, he continued living a sort of monastic life with a community of priests and others, and for nearly forty years he would be a driving force in the Church in North Africa. He would be called on at least twice to defend the truths of the Catholic Church.

For all the stories of heroism in the early Church, many Christians were less than heroic, denying their Christianity rather than facing death. By such denials, their lives were usually spared. After the early persecutions ceased, many people in the Church questioned whether the compromisers should be readmitted. Two schools of thought emerged. One held that bishops had the power to absolve such a transgression, though the penance should be severe. Others felt no readmission was possible.

The dispute arose again during the persecutions of Diocletian, this time more intensely. Unique to this persecution was an order given to bishops and priests to turn over to the government to be burned all copies of the Scriptures and other devotional works. Some questioned whether those who did so could be readmitted. In North Africa, a bishop named Donatus took the lead in denying the right of readmission to those clerics who had acquiesced. Around Donatus a separate church quickly emerged, not differing greatly from the Catholic Church in liturgy, sacraments, and the like. Within a short time each diocese in North Africa had both a Catholic bishop and a Donatist bishop, a Catholic Church and a Donatist church.

Augustine, quite naturally, found himself at the center of this raging controversy. He had to explain to the Donatists the Church's understanding of the sacrament of Holy Orders and, especially, the authority it conveyed. A man's personal weakness or sinfulness could not remove his commission to lead, since that authority came from Christ. Such bishops and priests who had failed in one important instance, he reminded them, still had the indelible character the sacrament bestowed and could continue to shepherd their flock. Even though Donatism was officially condemned at Carthage in 411, Augustine himself was never completely successful in stamping it out. Possidius, a member of Augustine's monastic community and later a fellow African bishop, leaves us a contemporary account:

> The Donatists ... whether they lived at Hippo or a neighboring town, used to bring his sermons and notes taken at them to their bishops.... After studying their answers, he would patiently and gently and, as is written, with fear and trembling, work for the salvation of all ... by showing that

those bishops were not willing or able to refute him and how true and evident on the contrary are the things which the faith of God's church holds and teaches. All this he did perseveringly day and night. . . . But these men were not confident of their own cause and were never willing even to answer him; instead they vented their anger and loudly claimed in private and in public that he was a seducer and deceiver of souls, they would say and preach that in defense of the flock he must be killed.[5]

For all its seriousness, Donatism affected only a limited area. No sooner had it been subdued than a far more encompassing heresy came upon the scene and spread quickly: Pelagianism, which took its name from a highly regarded British monk named Pelagius. He had distinguished himself not as an academic, but rather as a spiritual director. Rome thought well of him and would never have expected the legacy he would leave.

Pelagius focused on the supremacy of the human will and believed man was perfectly capable in himself of avoiding evil as well as doing it. He rejected the notion of Original Sin, the doctrine that we are the weak victims of concupiscence even after sin's remission. True, the sin of Adam was a violation of God's law, but it was a sin that affected only Adam, not his posterity. If a person is going to commit evil, he will do so of his own accord; conversely, he will avoid it of his own accord. No one has need of grace or divine assistance in the avoidance of sin; the human will is all sufficient. If Pelagius were correct, our Lord's Incarnation and subsequent redemption of man would be robbed of significance.

[5] John E. Rotelle, O.S.A., ed., *The Life of Saint Augustine by Possidius, Bishop of Calama* (Villanova, Pa.: Augustinian Press, 1988), 55.

Saint Augustine put a tremendous effort into what are known as his anti-Pelagian writings. He spent many years trying to prove the point that our wills need to be strengthened interiorly by God's grace. As one essayist summarizes the matter:

> Augustine was convinced that all human will had to be strengthened from within. . . . All the good things we do are gifts of divine grace. It seemed to him that the Pelagian claim to be able to achieve a church without spot or blemish continued the Donatist presumption of a pure church. In Augustine's eyes, the human situation is much more complex. Human freedom is not a static quality. Our freedom is always in a state of becoming: human freedom is by nature a limited freedom which has to become more and more free. Augustine also believed in the doctrine of original sin, including the existence of a collective guilt, with [man] kind as a whole responsible for the evil in the world.[6]

Pelagius was officially condemned at an Eastern Church council in Antioch in 418. With this, he disappears from history, though his teachings had influenced many. Some theologians felt Augustine may have gone a bit too far in refuting Pelagius, making everything dependent on God's grace and very little on human cooperation with God. The Second Council of Orange in 529 decided on a modified version of Augustine's view, emphasizing an absolute need for God's grace to do any salutary good, but also recognizing the necessity of human cooperation to accept God's grace.

In the course of his life, Augustine did far more than refute the Donatists and Pelagians. He developed a new and

---

[6] Tarcisius van Bavel, O.S.A., *Augustine* (Strasbourg: Éditions du Signe, 1996), 16.

unique theological position, not simply one that built upon earlier thought. By his death in 430, he had conceived a complete synthesis on the original state of creation, what the fall of man means, how the redemptive work of Jesus Christ transformed the course of salvation history, and how that same Christ continues to work in the lives of those he redeemed. The overwhelming majority of his works have found their way into the mainstream of Catholic theology:

> To the Catholics of his own day St. Augustine was the great champion of the church against the Manichees, the Donatists, the Pelagians. To the Catholic of a day fifteen hundred years later, he is still the Doctor of Grace and Ecclesiology. . . . But to Catholics of the thousand years which followed his death he was more than all this. He was almost the whole intellectual patrimony of medieval Catholicism, a mine of thought and erudition which the earlier Middle Ages, for all its delving, never came near to exhausting. He was the bridge between two worlds, and over that bridge there came to the Catholic Middle Ages . . . the tradition of its philosophy and all the riches of Christian Antiquity.[7]

---

[7] Hughes, *History of the Church*, 2:20–21.

III

The Triumph of Catholic Intelligence: Bonaventure, Albert the Great, and Thomas Aquinas

The Middle Ages, broadly defined, encompass the years 600–1300. The final century, the thirteenth, was the one in which Christendom was at its most powerful. Not only was faith strong, but the Church's influence seemed to permeate all aspects of culture. It is true that things such as the Inquisition and the Crusades had their dark sides, but contrasted with a political, social, educational, and moral order otherwise so strongly reflective of the gospel ethic, the overall picture is positive. That picture is still admired by many people in the twenty-first century.

One historian's observation that the thirteenth century was the "triumph of the Catholic intelligence"[1] seems particularly poignant. The first monumental event was the Fourth Lateran Council of 1215. Bishops, abbots, and religious superiors attended in the hundreds and decreed that Catholics must go to Confession and receive Holy Communion at least

---

[1] Philip Hughes, *A History of the Church* (New York: Sheed and Ward, 1949), 2:412.

once a year. They also defined transubstantiation, telling the faithful that once the words of Consecration are pronounced over the accidents of bread and wine by a validly ordained priest at Holy Mass, their substance is changed into the Body, Blood, Soul, and Divinity of Jesus Christ.

This was also the century when the "eldest daughter of the Church", France, was governed by a future saint, Louis IX, who gave succor to the Church and defined a Christian monarch's relationship to his people. Near the end of the century, Boniface VIII was elected Pope and presided over the Church's first jubilee, the Great Jubilee of 1300. Estimates of one million pilgrims visiting the Eternal City that year point to its spiritual success, a success further underscored by Boniface's strong statements on what would later be known as "the separation of church and state". As Supreme Pontiff, Boniface has rightly been described as the "ideal example of the achievement of the popes of that era".[2]

The great mendicant orders had their beginnings in these years as well: the Franciscans, founded by Francis of Assisi, and the Dominicans, established by Dominic Guzmán. The world of literature saw Dante Alighieri's *Divine Comedy*, a kaleidoscopic vision of hell, purgatory, and heaven that has become classic literature. Gothic cathedrals dotted the European landscape, science was enhanced through the work of the Franciscan Roger Bacon, and artistic masterpieces became commonplace.

More than anything, the thirteenth century was the century of education, especially centered in the university. The rise of a great school of theology at Paris as well as Bologna's law school are the earliest examples. They were followed by

---

[2] Alan Schreck, *The Compact History of the Catholic Church* (Ann Arbor, Mich.: Servant Books, 1987), 49.

the great universities of Oxford, Cambridge, Naples, and Sala-manca. In a certain sense, the thirteenth century parallels the twentieth. Prior to the Second World War, university education (especially in the United States) was very often limited to those of fairly affluent means or those preparing for the priesthood. With the passage of the "G.I. Bill", the United States experienced a tremendous increase in college and university enrollment, not to mention a knowledge explosion of staggering proportion. In much the same way, thirteenth-century universities had their antecedents in the eleventh-century cathedral schools and the emerging "guilds of scholars", which would eventually evolve into the university. An educational milieu strongly attracting eleventh-century clerics was greatly expanded by the thirteenth century with the translation of Aristotle's philosophical works into Latin and the interest in trying to incorporate philosophical inquiry into the study of theology, long the "queen of the sciences". The three theologians who attempted this came from the new religious orders: Bonaventure, from the Franciscans, and Albert the Great and Thomas Aquinas, from the Dominicans. They were the thirteenth century's defenders of the faith, and their contributions have been summed up succinctly:

St. Bonaventure continued the long tradition of a mystical approach to theology, while employing reason subordinated to the authority of tradition and faith. Albert the Great was one of the first great supporters of the thought of Aristotle, which had been initially banned by Rome from the universities because of it pagan origins. Albert's most renowned student, Thomas Aquinas, vigorously defended the value of Aristotle and constructed a system of thought that combined the Bible, the Church fathers, and Aristotelian reasoning into a great, unified system of understanding the

Christian revelation as a whole through faith enlightened by reason.[3]

Giovanni Fidanza, who as a Franciscan would become Bonaventure, was born in the medieval town of Bagnoregio in central Italy in 1221, just five years before the death of his order's founder, Saint Francis of Assisi. His background was very Franciscan. Alexander of Hales, the first Franciscan Doctor, had Bonaventure as a student at the University of Paris. The student would become a professor at the same university (having first obtained a licentiate) and spend the next seven years producing much of the scholarly work for which he is remembered. His selection as Minister General of the order of Friars Minor would bring many of his scholarly efforts to a close as he focused more on administrative tasks.

Bonaventure's years at the University of Paris, while productive, were not always tranquil. There were several schools of philosophical thought represented, and Aristotelianism was particularly strong. Those disciples of Aristotle had a strong fear of other trends becoming too prevalent, especially those of the Franciscans, who were little influenced by Aristotelian metaphysics. The factual debate became so intense, the Pope was forced to intervene. He reasserted the Franciscans' right to teach at the university and appointed Bonaventure the official occupant of the order's theological chair.

The Seraphic Doctor, as he has become known, believed that the study of philosophy could be very useful in unraveling theological truths, but useful only insofar as it aided his approach of presenting the whole of an earthly life as a journey to God, who is always the object of one's love. This had to be done in a language every man could understand; if

[3] Ibid., 54.

man could grasp the infinitely lovable God, he could then be persuaded to give a strong assent of faith. The knowledge of God one obtained through faith was a more concrete reality than anything philosophy could provide through reason.

The Franciscans had a strong pietistic tradition dating to their founder. Bonaventure's approach to philosophy underscores this and makes Francis' thought come alive. Though we are the weakened victims of Original Sin and see God only dimly, by being sufficiently attentive and using reason to enliven our faith, we are able to perceive God all around us, and if we truly want to find him, we need to look no further than our own souls.

> God is equally discernable to every man, in his own soul if he will but look into it. Here it is not a mere reflection of God that meets the believer's gaze, not a mere trace of His power, but His very image. For the idea of God is bound up with the very simplest of our intellectual operations. Unless the idea of a self-existing being were present to the mind, man could not know anything. The image of God is naturally infused into the soul, and whoever will gaze into its depths must find God.[4]

Bonaventure's life was not limited to the halls of academe. His administrative, pastoral, and negotiating skills were put to work for the good of the order with his appointment as Minister General during a period of internal crisis in 1257. At no time, however, did he lose interest in scholarly debate or the progress of his thought, which was kept alive by his students. Monsignor Philip Hughes, a distinguished Church historian of some years ago, attempts to situate Bonaventure's contribution in the scheme of things:

[4] Hughes, *History of the Church*, 2:416.

Saint Bonaventure's doctrine had the advantage ... that it was first in the field. Also, it was in keeping with the spirit that so far characterized, not merely the Franciscan school at Paris, but the general theological teaching of the university. It was ... a faithful critique of the new philosophical world in the spirit of Saint Augustine, and it reflected all the Platonic spirit that showed in the greatest of the Fathers himself.[5]

Born a generation earlier than Bonaventure was a German Dominican known in his own time as Albert, and ever since as Albert the Great. A fellow Dominican commentator noted:

When Albert died in 1280 he was already something of a legend. Even in his own lifetime, contrary to all normal academic etiquette, he was being treated as an "authority" in the schools, on a par with the ancients; and a Dominican preacher in Paris could refer with evident proprietary satisfaction to *our* philosopher. . . . Albert's friend, fellow Dominican and pupil, Ulrich of Strasbourg, describes him as "so godlike (*divinus*) in every branch of knowledge that he can aptly be called the wonder and the miracle of our time".[6]

Albert's exact date of birth is doubtful, but was surely at the end of the twelfth century. A native German, son of a vassal of the Emperor, he was exposed to education early on at the University of Padua in Italy. There he was strongly influenced by the great mathematician Jordan of Saxony, successor to Saint Dominic as Minister General of the Order of Friars Preachers. Jordan was equally known as an eloquent and persuasive preacher and could have been the catalyst drawing Albert into the Dominican order.

[5] Ibid., 418.

[6] Simon Tugwell, O.P., ed., *Albert and Thomas: Selected Writings* (New York: Paulist Press, 1988), 3.

It may sound presumptuous to claim Albert's knowledge of the world to have been as great as Aristotle's, but that is a claim many scholars of Albert would make. It was the natural world that fascinated him, and he read voraciously all the multidisciplinary literature coming into Western Europe from Greek and Arab sources. He would be recompensed more than adequately for his years of personal study:

> The real honor paid to Albert by the order was the decision that he should lecture ... [at the University of] Paris, with a view to becoming a Master in Theology. At this time Paris was the only international study house that the Dominicans had, and even to be sent there as an ordinary student was no mean privilege, seeing that each province was only allowed to send three students there a year. But the chances of becoming a Master were even more restricted.[7]

Albert's study of the natural world included much concentration on physics as well as the other secular sciences, which was opportune due to the thirteenth century's dialogue between the natural and supernatural disciplines. No sooner had Albert begun lecturing at the University of Paris than the uniqueness of his style and the novelty and depth of his presentation became apparent. The city's lecture halls could not contain the numbers desiring to hear him, so he often lectured in the open air. One such locale became known as the Place Maubert, a name which itself is a corruption of the Place Maître Albert:

> In St. Albert ... there appears for the first time what so far the intellectual development of the Middle Ages had lacked, namely, a view of knowledge as a whole, related to the whole

[7] Ibid., 9.

universe of fact and experience. He is not just another commentator, the best equipped so far. His work is a new explanation of the universe, made in Aristotle's spirit, and according to Aristotle's method. But the explanation is St. Albert's and it won him, immediately, the rare distinction that his books were used as texts. For the schools of his own day St. Albert ranked, with Aristotle himself, as an authority.[8]

One of his great services was the clear distinction he made between the very separate disciplines of philosophy and theology. Reason is something one naturally associates with the more secular philosophical approach to knowledge, yet Albert was quick to point out how helpful reason could be to theology, the study of the supernatural. What is important in Albert's thought is the limitation he places on reason. Reason is not Godlike, but helps us in our understanding of God. In that pursuit, one encounters mystery, and reason must give way to faith, and faith to love. Much like his Franciscan counterpart, Bonaventure, Albert also believed that in this life God could not be perceived directly, only a trace of him was discernable to the human intellect.

It was as a writer and teacher that Albert made his most notable contributions, but again, like Bonaventure, he was not exclusively an academic. He "was always a preacher and a priest as well." [9] And with this in mind, he was sent to organize the studies of his order in Cologne, where one may still visit his tomb in the Dominican church, just a short walk from the city's magnificent cathedral.

At one point, while Albert was still teaching in Paris, an aristocratic young Neapolitan was sent to join the local com-

---

[8] Hughes, *History of the Church*, 2:420.
[9] Tugwell, *Albert and Thomas*, 35.

munity by the General of the order. This idea was to put the young man beyond the reach of his family, whose ambitions for him were devastated by his desire to become a Dominican and who had resorted to all possible means to divert him from his chosen path. His name was Tomasso d'Aquino. He arrived in Paris in 1246 and seems to have attached himself rather quickly to Master Albert. Tomasso was a reserved, quiet young man, whom his Dominican brethren nicknamed "Dumb Ox"; but bit by bit his talent emerged, and Albert is said to have commented one day, "You call him a Dumb Ox; I tell you this Dumb Ox shall bellow so loud that his bellowings will fill the world." [10]

This man was, of course, Thomas Aquinas. G. K. Chesterton in his classic study of him noted:

> An acute observer said of Thomas Aquinas in his own time, "He could alone restore all philosophy, if it had been burnt by fire." That is what is meant by saying that he was an original man, a creative mind; that he could have made his own cosmos out of stones and straws, even without the manuscripts of Aristotle or Augustine. [11]

Saint Thomas was born in 1225 in the ancestral castle Roccasecca, located midway between Rome and Naples. His background was similar to Albert the Great's. He was the son of the Count of Aquino (who himself was a first cousin of Emperor Henry VI); his paternal grandmother was the sister of Frederick Barbarosa. Thomas' family was, therefore, a noble one, and among his father's titles was Baron of the Kingdom of Sicily.

---

[10] G. K. Chesterton, *St. Thomas Aquinas* (San Francisco: Ignatius Press, 2002), 67. See also Tugwell, *Albert and Thomas*, 11.

[11] Chesterton, *St. Thomas Aquinas*, 126.

Thomas spent nine years of his young life in the Benedictine monastery of Monte Cassino, and upon finishing his studies he went to the newly established University of Naples. When he offered himself in 1244 as a novice to the Order of Friars Preachers, his brother, disturbed by his obvious waste of talent to the secular world, kidnapped him and locked him in the dungeon of Roccasecca. There he remained for a year, with only the Bible and Aristotle to read. In 1245, as the story goes, the Pope intervened and said Thomas should be allowed to follow his vocation. Between Paris and Cologne, Thomas was to spend over a decade studying for degrees and coming under the tutelage of Albert.

The Angelic Doctor's earthly life did not complete fifty years. That he was able to produce the volume of work he did is a sure testimony to God's grace. Generally his works are grouped in three categories: his commentaries on philosophy and Scripture; his theological works, namely the *Summa contra Gentiles* and the *Summa Theologica*; and the mass of miscellaneous writings and treatises on special questions. The way in which all of these works developed has been the subject of at least one historian's interest:

> His tranquil, ordered mind never ceased to grow, and, despite the racket of the never ceasing controversy, it grew in ordered peace. As a writer he is impersonality itself. . . . All is set down in a cold, clear style where the words are wrung dry of any but the exact meaning they are chosen to express. The poetry of his soul, its never ceasing aspiration to God, the fire of his love for God—these things are only to be discerned in the saint's clear exposition of the truth whence they all derived.[12]

---

[12] Hughes, *History of the Church*, 2:424.

Saint Thomas surely knew controversy in his life, but he did not write the *Summa Theologica* as a work of refutation. Rather, he wished to tell the entire story of God and the universe he created as the Church understands it through Scripture, tradition, and the use of reason. Aquinas was not the most widely read philosopher of his day (John Duns Scotus supposedly had a larger following), but no one captured God, the Divine Intelligence, in quite the same way. In an amazingly logical and sequential pattern, Thomas traces man's creation and fall from grace and the tremendous events enabling creatures to return to God, namely, the Incarnation of Christ, his subsequent Redemption of the world, the Church he established, the sacraments he gave to his Church, and the grace he continually bestows on men as the most vital means to achieve their eternal salvation. All of this Thomas accomplishes in a tremendously optimistic fashion for all generations:

> [T]he whole vast panorama of Revelation is surveyed scientifically and rationally. The *Summa Theologica* is the greatest book ever written. It has about it the eternity of the metaphysical. It is as relevant today as it was to those who first read and studied in it.[13]

The faith was, therefore, well defended in the thirteenth century by Bonaventure, Albert the Great, and Thomas, each in his own way. This was not a period in which entire nations were being swept away with heresy. It was, rather, a century in which timeless truths were developed for succeeding generations, in cooperation with secular science, insofar as possible. These men could engage the world because they

---

[13] Ibid., 429.

understood the world's thinking; they could defend the faith because they understood even more clearly the limitations of the world's thinking. Nearly eight centuries later, the Church reaps the benefit of their labors and thanks God for their lives.

IV

The Counter-Reformation: Ignatius and the Jesuits

On October 31, 1517, an Augustinian monk named Martin Luther, long fearful for his own salvation, seemed to unleash tremendous personal hostility when he nailed his famous Ninety-five Theses to the door of the cathedral in Wittenburg, Germany. This single action has traditionally been viewed as the beginning of the Protestant Reformation. Before it ended, several new theologies were formulated by at least two generations of reformers, causing Christianity to fall into centuries of division.

The term *sola fide* ("faith alone") is often associated with Luther. It was a belief that provided him a great deal of inner tranquility. Once, while meditating on Saint Paul's Letter to the Romans, Luther came to the verse that states that "man is justified by faith apart from works of the law." [1] Luther took this to mean that a person does not have the capability to work out his own salvation because of his sinful human nature. Instead, God gives his free gift of grace, which stimulates faith and leads to salvation. Luther rejected, it appears,

---

[1] Rom 3:28.

the admonition of the Apostle James that faith without good works is dead,[2] preferring to concentrate only on that which gave him inner peace.

Luther also opposed the buying and selling of indulgences, a practice quite rampant in the western Europe of his day. The Church has always taught that an indulgence is a remission of the temporal punishment due to sin, and Luther correctly pointed out that such forgiveness cannot be purchased. The abuse of selling indulgences and the erroneous attitudes it created are well illustrated by the slogan of a preacher in Luther's time: "Another soul to heaven springs when in the box a shilling rings." [3]

While justification and indulgences are the issues for which Luther is best remembered, many more grievances comprised his Wittenburg list. Some two years after he had posted them, he confided in writing to a friend that the idea of the Pope as the anti-Christ, once repellent to him, now seemed to have more plausibility. Luther at first had no intention of beginning a new ecclesial body. As he meditated on Scripture, however, he began to think that the Church should return to the gospel in its purest form as he envisioned it, eliminating what he regarded as unnecessary liturgical ceremony, hierarchical structure, and the like:

> For Luther everything began from his fundamental experience . . . salvation comes [to human beings] from God through faith alone. God does everything and they do nothing. Good works do not make people good, but once people have been justified by God they do good works. . . . So Luther turned his back on everything in tradition which denied the pre-

[2] James 2:17.
[3] Jean Comby with Diarmaid MacCulloch, *How to Read Church History* (New York: Crossroad, 1991), 2:11.

eminence of scripture and faith. He rejected what appeared to him as a means, a claim on the human side to deserve salvation: the cult of the saints, indulgences, religious vows, those sacraments which [he could not find] attested in the New Testament. Anything not explicitly set out in scripture was worthless. All that counted was the universal priesthood of the faithful.[4]

In 1520, the papal bull *Exsurge* formally condemned forty-one of Luther's propositions, and he was given two months to submit to the authority of the Church. In December 1520, he publicly burned his copy of *Exsurge*, and excommunication followed one month later.

Closely akin to Luther was Ulrich Zwingli in Switzerland. A former priest and student of the Renaissance scholar Erasmus, Zwingli was based in the city of Zurich, having moved from Glavis, the scene of his former priestly labors. He was, from all accounts, a more inwardly secure man than Luther. His preoccupation was not so much his own eternal destiny as it was freeing his disciples from the shackles of Rome's domination. Following this view and a Lutheran disposition toward "gospel purity", reformed churches were established in Switzerland. These congregations established vernacular liturgies, in contrast to the Latin liturgy of the Catholic Church. They also removed statues of the saints, secularized convents, and followed other practices emerging in neighboring Germany.

The French layman John Calvin brought a nonclerical background to Reformation theology and represented a younger generation of reformers. Calvin was also based in Switzerland, though in the city of Geneva. In fact, his grave can

---

[4] Ibid., 13.

be seen there to this day. It consists of a single pole, atop of which are the initials "J. C." This protrudes through some greenery and is surrounded by a small iron fence. The grave is reminiscent of the stark nature of ecclesial architecture in Calvinistic churches, if not the severity of Calvin's thought.

Calvin was obsessed with the sovereign nature of God. In his *Institutes of the Christian Religion*, he develops the theory for which he is best remembered: predestination. All creatures merited damnation, but God in his mercy chose some for salvation. These, in turn, needed the vehicle of a church in which to express their faith. Calvin's emphasis was very much on the church as a local community of believers in whom power rested. His unique brand of theology was gradually adopted by religious groups identified as Presbyterians, Huguenots, Puritans, and Congregationalists. His ideas spread quickly to England and to its colonies in North America. Also, they found their way to Scotland in the person of John Knox, as well as the Low Countries of Europe, Holland in particular.

In England, despite the fact that Henry VIII was given the title Defender of the Faith by the Holy See for a book published under his name, the monarch was anything but a theologian, and the Reformation in England was not theological in origin. Henry's wife Catherine of Aragon gave him no male heirs. Wishing to have his marriage annulled, but refused by the Church, he turned to the English clergy with the same request and subsequently declared himself head of the church in England. Henry's Six Articles, promulgated in 1539, kept the essentials of the Catholic faith (even though failure to take the Act of Supremacy recognizing Henry's headship of the church led most often to execution). It was not until his death that Calvinistic theology began to find its way into the Book of Common Prayer. When Henry's daughter Mary Tudor became monarch in 1553, she briefly restored Catholicism and carried out over two hundred executions of Protestant heretics. Upon the accession of her half-sister Elizabeth (the daughter of Henry VIII and Anne Boleyn), Anglicanism was officially established as the state religion and the Thirty-nine Articles spelled out the particulars of belief. They did not rid the Church of England of as many vestiges of Romanism as some would have liked. It seemed to be

> a theology very close to neighbouring Calvinism which maintained traditional forms like the episcopate and liturgical vestments. Both Catholic and Protestant dissidents were mercilessly persecuted.[5]

The Reformation was, to be sure, no isolated event, but a series of movements in several European countries that in varying ways departed from Catholicism. In response to Protestantism and to the problems it sought to address, the Catholic renewal or Counter-Reformation became a reality. One of the magnificent fruits of that renewal was the establishment of the Society of Jesus, founded by the Spanish Basque Ignatius of Loyola.

Loyola is a castle at Azpeitia, located in the Pyrenees Mountains. It was there that Iñigo, as he was then called, was born, in 1491. His background was military, and he fought briefly against the French in Pamplona. A serious battle injury brought him back to his native castle and confined him for weeks. He was a worldly sort and would love to have occupied his hours reading romantic novels. Instead, only two books, on the lives of the saints and the life of Christ, were available. The biographies of the saints began to fascinate

[5] Ibid., 21.

him, make him think of the uselessness of his own life up to that point, and provoked the interior question: If such acts of spiritual heroism were possible in the lives of others, why would they not be possible in his?

A hunger for God began to overtake him by degrees, and after a time he resolved to go on pilgrimage to the shrine of Our Lady of Montserrat. Sometime during the course of that visit he determined that thenceforth he would lead a penitential life and his stay in the nearby small town of Manresa, where he experienced solitude and prayer, confirmed his desire all the more. He made a pilgrimage to the Holy Land and then studied in Barcelona, Alcala, and, finally, at the University of Paris, where he received the Master of Arts in 1534. Still his fervor did not slacken. At Paris he was to meet companions who were like-minded in spiritual outlook and whose names would become well known in Jesuit annals: Francis Xavier (a Spanish Basque like Ignatius), Favre, Laynez, Salmeron, Rodriguez, Bobadilla. Together they would become "the Company", the first Jesuits, defenders of the faith in heretical times.

On the feast of Our Lady's Assumption, August 15, 1534, these men professed their vows in the chapel of Saint Denis on the hill of Montmartre in Paris. They vowed to work for the glory of God. They agreed that when they finished their studies and became priests, they would go to Jerusalem together, but if they could not go there in a year, they would go to Rome and offer to go anywhere the Pope deemed necessary. Their hopes of going to Palestine would not be realized, but other needs quickly became apparent.

There being no likelihood of their being able soon to go to the Holy Land, it was at length resolved that Ignatius, Favre, and Laynez should go to Rome and offer the services of all to the pope, and they agreed that if anyone asked what their association was they might answer "the Company of Jesus", because they were united to fight against falsehood and vice under the standard of Christ. On his road to Rome, praying at a little chapel at La Storta, Ignatius saw our Lord, shining with an unspeakable light, but loaded with a heavy cross, and he heard the words, *Ego vobis Romae propitius ero*, "I will be favorable to you at Rome."[6]

Eventually they became a religious order and took formal vows. The members of the Society of Jesus, or Jesuits, truly were men of the Church. The papal bull of institution, promulgated in 1540 during the pontificate of Pope Paul III, stated the Society's purposes. The document "Rules for Thinking with the Church" is also illustrative. It was composed by Ignatius himself as an addition to his *Spiritual Exercises*. It represents a reply to the Protestant challenge, affirming many long-established practices that were under severe criticism and attack. It is a document "characterized more perhaps by its balance and moderation than one may at first think".[7] Rule Thirteen initially appears anything but moderate:

> If we wish to proceed securely in all things, we must hold fast to the following principle: What seems to me white, I will believe black if the hierarchical Church so defines. For I must be convinced that in Christ Our Lord, the bridegroom, and in His spouse the Church, only one Spirit holds sway, which governs and rules for the salvation of souls. For it is by the same Spirit and Lord who gave the Ten

[6] Herbert Thurston, S.J., and Donald Attwater, eds., *Butler's Lives of the Saints* (Westminster, Md.: Christian Classics, 1988), 3:224.

[7] John C. Olin, *The Catholic Reformation: Savonarola to Ignatius Loyola* (New York: Harper and Row, 1969), 202.

Commandments that our Holy Mother Church is ruled and governed.[8]

In addition to absolute loyalty, Ignatius in the *Constitutions* leaves no doubt that it is to be interpreted as willingness to carry out the wishes of the Holy See:

> All that His Holiness will command us for the good of souls, or the propagation of the faith, we are bound to carry out with neither procrastination nor excuse, at once and to the fullest extent of our power, whether he sends us among the Turks, to the New Worlds, to the Lutherans, or any other manner of believers or unbelievers. . . . This vow may scatter us to the distant parts of the world.[9]

The work of the Jesuits in defending the faith must be looked at in the context of the Counter-Reformation. The times called for a spirited defense of faith; it was the time for Catholic renewal; the Church had been weakened from within by the laxity of her own; she had been weakened from without by the strong theological dissent of the various reformers. The Church had to respond adequately, and the Jesuits found themselves part of this response. In all manner of response, however, Ignatius was quite insistent that charity prevail and that the integrity of the Church not suffer because of the misdeeds or poorly contrived statements of those attempting to defend it:

> Great care must be taken to show forth orthodox truth in such a way that if any heretics happen to be present they may have an example of charity and Christian moderation. No

---

[8] *The Spiritual Exercises of St. Ignatius*, trans. Louis J. Puhl, S.J. (Chicago: Loyola University Press, 1951), 160.

[9] Jean Lacouture, *Jesuits: A Multibiography* (Washington, D.C.: Counterpoint, 1995), 76.

hard words should be used nor any sort of contempt for their errors be shown.[10]

A man can be charitable as he clearly, unambiguously teaches Catholic truth. This was Ignatius' aim, and education was to play a key role. If men were adequately trained, the Church would be better served; such motivated the opening of the Roman and German colleges in the Eternal City. The former was established primarily though the largesse of the family of Saint Francis Borgia, the man who would become Ignatius' successor as third General of the Society; the latter was an educational bastion for students from all countries affected by the Reformation.

Although an educated Jesuit was always to exercise charity, his response to heresy must be firm and decisive. One of the truly great Jesuits to receive instruction from Ignatius before undertaking his mission was Saint Peter Canisius:

> Once a man has been convicted of heretical impiety or is strongly suspect of it, he has no right to any honour or riches: on the contrary, these must be stripped from him ... If public professors or administrators at the University of Vienna or the other universities have a bad reputation in relation to the Catholic faith, they must be deprived of their degrees. All heretical books must be burned, or sent beyond all the provinces of the kingdom.[11]

Canisius' record of educational beginnings is impressive: Ingolstadt, Vienna, Prague, Strasbourg in Alsace (where he was involved in the opening negotiations), Innsbruck (where he introduced the Sodality of the Blessed Virgin Mary to

---

[10] Thurston and Attwater, *Butler's Lives of the Saints*, 3:225–26.

[11] Ignatius of Loyola to Peter Canisius, August 13, 1554, cited in Comby and MacCulloch, *How to Read Church History*, 2:30.

collegians), Dillingen, and Fribourg. In addition, he managed time at the Council of Trent, where his very practical advice to the Council Fathers about the Reformation in Germany was highly regarded. Strong as his defense of Catholicism was in day-to-day relations with German Protestants, he favored the approach of peaceful coexistence. Some saw this as betrayal, but Canisius felt (and later convinced Rome) that a calm, firm, and educated approach would help Catholics win an intellectual battle they had previously been losing. All of this is not to suggest that his career was solely academically oriented. His sojourn in Vienna proves the contrary:

> Many parishes were without clergy, and the Jesuits had to supply the lack as well as to teach in their newly-founded college. Not a single priest had been ordained for twenty years; monasteries lay desolate; members of the religious orders were jeered at in the streets; nine-tenths of the inhabitants had abandoned the faith, while the few who still regarded themselves as Catholics had, for the most part, ceased to practise their religion. At first Peter Canisius preached to almost empty churches, partly because of the general disaffection and partly because his Rhineland German grated on the ears of the Viennese; but he found his way to the heart of the people by his indefatigable ministrations to the sick and dying during an outbreak of the plague. The energy and enterprise of the man was astounding; he was concerned about everything and everybody, from lecturing in the university to visiting the neglected criminals in the jails.[12]

Such accomplishments could, no doubt, have been recounted in any of the cities where Canisius spent any length of time. Christopher Hollis, in his study of the Jesuits, sums

[12] Thurston and Attwater, *Butler's Lives of the Saints*, 2:168–69.

up the work of this saint, now venerated as a Doctor of the Church:

> The general effect of Canisius' work was immense. He turned the course of history. In each of the great colleges he built there were up to a thousand students. He was the first Jesuit to enter Poland. By 1600, there were 466 Jesuits there. When he entered Germany in 1550, he entered with 2 Jesuits as his companions. When he left it over 30 years later there were 1,111 Jesuits at work in the country.[13]

Germany was, of course, not the only scene of the Reformation. Jesuits labored in many countries on the Continent, and also in England. Even before the English mission was a reality, Ignatius ordered prayers for the conversion of England and for the English and Welsh martyrs of penal times, twenty-six of whom had been Jesuits. Centuries later Henry Edward Manning, Cardinal Archbishop of Westminster, himself a convert to Catholicism (and from his tone no particular friend of the Reformation), wrote about the work of the English Jesuits:

> It was exactly what was wanted at the time to counteract the revolt of the sixteenth century. The revolt was disobedience and disorder in the most aggressive form. The Society was obedience and order in the most solid compactness. . . . They also won back souls by their preaching and spiritual guidance. They preached 'Jesus Christ and Him crucified'. This had been their central message, and by it they have deserved and won the confidence and obedience of souls.[14]

[13] Christopher Hollis, *The Jesuits: A History* (New York: Macmillan Company, 1968), 25.

[14] Thurston and Attwater, *Butler's Lives of the Saints*, 3:225.

Jesuit missionary activity was strongly influenced by two sources: Ignatius' *Spiritual Exercises* and the *Imitation of Christ* by Thomas a Kempis. The Society's founder tried to induce in the life of each Jesuit a peaceful state of mind without inordinate attachments. Such inner tranquility would help one in moments of crisis and in the major decisions of life. With a peaceful mind, each of life's situations could be assessed in the light of God's glory and the salvation of one's immortal soul. The *Imitation* spoke to the heart of the disciple and always tried to elicit a generous response. It is in this context that all Jesuit renewal should be judged. British historian Thomas Macaulay, writing in grand style, captures these grand men:

> The order possessed itself once of all the strongholds which command the public mind, of the pulpit, of the press, of the confessional, of the academies. Wherever the Jesuit preached, the church was too small for the audience. The name of a Jesuit on a title-page secured the circulation of a book. It was in the ears of a Jesuit that the powerful, the noble, the beautiful, breathed the secret history of their lives. It was at the feet of the Jesuit that the youth of the higher and middle class were brought up from childhood to manhood.[15]

It was to be the lot of Ignatius to spend most of his Jesuit life in Rome, so vast an undertaking was it to direct the Society's business. He saw the Society of Jesus grow from the original company to one thousand members in nine countries and provinces in Europe, India, and Brazil. His death came suddenly on July 31, 1556, in Rome. One may still see the room, along with the adjoining quarters, where he wrote his So-

---

[15] Thomas Macaulay, *Essay on Von Rank's History of the Papacy*, cited in Hollis, *Jesuits*, 27.

ciety's *Constitutions*. His tomb is venerated in the magnificent church of the Gesù on Rome's famous Corso Vittorio Emmanuele. His was a life lived for Christ and in defense of his Church, or as one commentator has put it, "To gain others to Christ he made himself all things to all men, going in at *their* door and coming out at *his own*." [16]

[16] Thurston and Attwater, *Butler's Lives of the Saints*, 3:227.

V

Saint Charles Borromeo and the Reform of the Clergy

There is a temptation to view the Church of the sixteenth century as solely preoccupied with the Reformation. In fact, there was significant internal weakness; the light of faith had grown very dim in certain areas, and a new spiritual energy had to be kindled individually and collectively:

> Within the religious community itself there were ominous signs of weakness and disorder: . . . the worldliness and secularization of the hierarchy that reached to the papacy itself in the High Renaissance, ignorance and immorality among the lower clergy, laxity in monastic discipline, and spiritual decay in the religious life, theological desiccation and confusion, superstition and abuse in religious practice. The picture should not be overdrawn (there were many instances of sanctity, dedication, and even spiritual renewal during this time), but in general Catholic life in the late Middle Ages seemed grievously depressed.[1]

[1] John C. Olin, *The Catholic Reformation: Savonarola to Ignatius Loyola* (New York: Harper and Row, 1969), xv.

A moralistic-style poem, first published in Switzerland in the late fifteenth century, is even more poignant:

> Saint Peter's ship is swaying madly / It may be wrecked, or damaged badly / The waves are striking 'gainst the side / And storm and trouble may betide.[2]

Spiritual decline had taken its toll in the Church by the time the Protestant reformers had come to prominence. It was only when they officially departed the Church that many of her leaders began to see a clearer picture of internal problems. The difficulty was not so much the way people were thinking as the way they were living; viewed in this light the reformers had reformed the wrong things. If anything good may be said to have come out of the Reformation, it was the strengthening of Catholic doctrine and spiritual life. This took institutional form in the Council of Trent.

Trent is a northern Italian city not far from the Austrian border. As such, it was close to those areas deeply affected by the Reformation. Since much of its work had to do with reaffirming Catholic doctrine, Emperor Charles V felt the city's proximate location was ideal. The council met for three different time periods, each led by a different Pope: 1545–1547 (Pope Paul III), 1551–1552 (Pope Julius III), and 1562–1563 (Pope Pius IV). It adopted an entirely new system for the training of priests in special colleges, or seminaries. Such schools were designed to produce a better-educated, more moral, spiritual, and professionally conscious clergy. Great emphasis was placed on preaching and teaching, all the while insisting on the conscientious fulfillment of priestly and episcopal duties in later life. Priestly studies in the sixteenth

---

[2] Ibid., xvi.

century generally began at an early age, and the Council Fathers had this in mind when they noted:

> Unless young people are well educated, they can easily be led astray towards the pleasures of the world. Also, unless they are trained in piety and religion at the tenderest age, when vicious habits have not yet entirely taken ahold of them, it is impossible for them to persevere in a perfect fashion in church discipline without very great and special protection from Almighty God.[3]

Specific instruction was then given for the establishment of seminaries and the spiritual formation that was to be given in them. The ministerial priesthood received a tremendous shot of spiritual adrenaline from the documents of Trent. It had been vigorously attacked by several of the reformers and needed to be reaffirmed. Holy, ordained men were needed to serve as priests, since without the priesthood there is no Eucharist. Hence:

> If anyone says that there is no visible or external priesthood in the New Testament, or that there is no power to consecrate, to offer the true body and true blood of the Lord, and to forgive or retain sins . . . let them be anathema.[4]

One of the guiding forces in this priestly renewal was the nephew of Pope Pius IV, Charles Borromeo, a man who used all of his influence and energy to persuade his uncle to reconvene the Council of Trent and who, along with Ignatius of Loyola, Philip Neri, and Pope Saint Pius V, is remem-

---

[3] H. D. Bettenson, *Documents of the Christian Church*, cited in Jean Comby and Diarmaid MacCulloch, *How to Read Church History* (New York: Crossroad, 1991–1992), 2:28.

[4] Ibid.

bered as one of the "four outstanding public men of the . . . Counter-reformation".[5]

Charles was born on October 2, 1538, at the castle of Arona on Lake Maggiore. Born into an aristocratic family, he was the son of Count Gilbert Borromeo, a very devout Catholic gentleman, and Margaret de Medici, the daughter of a *nouveau riche* family of Milan. It was her younger brother who would become Pope Pius IV. As a young boy, Charles was a slow, serious student, one who might be described as severe. He showed a tremendous concern for the poor, which would become a lifelong preoccupation and allow him even as a boy to be conspicuously spiritually detached. He obtained a doctorate at the University of Pavia and returned to Milan in 1559 to the news that his uncle had been chosen Pope in the conclave following the death of Paul IV.

In the sixteenth century it was not at all uncommon for laymen or those in minor orders to be designated cardinals. The new Pope lost no time in so designating his twenty-three-year-old nephew, Charles, who while en route to the priesthood had taken only minor orders. Pius IV named him a cardinal deacon and appointed him administrator of the vacant see of Milan. In addition, he was named papal legate to Bologna and Romagna and cardinal protector of Portugal, the Low Countries, the Catholic Cantons of Switzerland, and the orders of Saint Francis, the Carmelites, the Knights of Malta, and others.

His life took him rather quickly to the Vatican, where he became known as a patron of the arts and a promoter of the same among the clergy. Also, he opened a literary academy for priests and laymen. These sorts of social settings lent

---

[5] Herbert Thurston, S.J., and Donald Attwater, eds., *Butler's Lives of the Saints* (Westminister, Md.: Christian Classics, 1988), 4:255.

themselves to a gracious lifestyle, but it was one that never impressed Charles. He seemed to feel the more grandiose the setting, the less meaning it had, so he led a remarkably simple life amid opulence. He once confided to an archbishop friend:

> You see my position. . . . You know what it is to be a Pope's nephew, and a nephew beloved by him; nor are you ignorant what it is to live in the court of Rome. The dangers are infinite. What ought I to do, young as I am, and without experience? God has given me ardour for penance; and I have some thoughts of going into a monastery, to live as if there were only God and myself in the world.[6]

The archbishop confidant tried to reassure Charles of his tremendous value to the Church, a value that might be far better utilized in his diocese. With that in mind, he should make every effort to go to Milan as soon as possible. While the advice was given in all sincerity, getting to Milan was not as easy as it might have been. Charles came from a large, prestigious family; the mere maintenance of family interests and holdings constituted full-time employment. When Charles' older brother, Count Frederick Borromeo, died, many family members and friends assumed that his younger sibling would abandon priestly aspirations, return to the family, marry, and concern himself with the many temporalities that needed constant attention. They were wrong. Ordination to the priesthood came for Charles in 1563, after he had placed all the family business in the hands of an uncle. His episcopal ordination followed his priestly ordination by only three months, but he was still hindered from going to his diocese.

[6] Ibid., 4:256.

Much of the work of the Catechism of the Council of Trent was his, so he was involved in its preparation for considerable time. There were liturgical books to be revised and collections of church music to be put in order. All of this involved work, and Charles could not leave until its completion. Even then, Pope Pius V was so dependent on the saintly Borromeo that he was extremely reluctant to release him. It was only after great persistence on Charles' part that papal approval for the return to Milan was granted. The Archbishop officially arrived in his see in April 1566, and he went to work vigorously for the spiritual reform of his diocese.

Milan had not had a resident archbishop for eighty years, and the condition of faith and morals could only be described as deplorable. Some years before Charles took up permanent residence, he appointed a vicar general, who, in turn, had sought the help of the Society of Jesus. Even with such Jesuit help, the vicar had met with limited success. Charles was able to make only one initial visit before permanently arriving. Calling a provincial council, he knew very well that it was just the beginning.

The city Charles arrived in, not to mention the archdiocese, was staggering. A nineteenth-century source gives details:

> On the north, towards Germany, the diocese extended more than a hundred miles in length, and it included not only the State of Milan, but part of Venice, of the Duchy of Monteferrato, and of Switzerland. Lofty mountains surrounded a great part of it. Two thousand two hundred and twenty churches were under the jurisdiction of the Archbishop.... The clergy numbered more than three thousand. The convents of women were seventy in number.... There were a hundred communities of men. The total number of souls contained in the diocese was computed to be at least six hundred thousand. The province comprised fifteen bishoprics,

embracing not only the State of Milan, but the whole of
Monteferrato, part of Venice and Piedmont, and the Ge-
noese Republic, and extended along the shores of the Med-
iterranean to the borders of Provence.[7]

Given conditions, Charles knew that nothing short of his
physical presence in the diocese would do. He would live in
Milan and work day in and day out in the midst of his people. Those who had remained fervent in faith were as much
in need of an increase in their spiritual fervor as were Catholics in many parts of western Europe. Milan was geograph-
ically close to centers of the Protestant Reformation, and
Catholic doctrine had become tainted. The Archbishop gave
top priority to the teaching of Catholic truth not only to
children but also to adults who had been exposed to ques-
tionable theology.

The reform of the clergy was vital. Significant numbers of
diocesan clergy did not live in parochial houses, dressed in
secular clothing, and even carried weapons. Many were involved in open, sinful relationships with women. Charles
found large numbers of priests who had not gone to Confession in years; they felt they had no need to since they
heard the confessions of others. Many could not even recite
the form of sacramental Absolution from memory. The academic and spiritual preparation for Holy Orders had been
extremely poor, and their lives reflected it. The situation had
become so pronounced that a humorously sarcastic observation was bandied about that if one wished to go to hell, one
need only become a priest.[8]

[7] John Peter Giussano, *The Life of Saint Charles Borromeo: Cardinal Archbishop of Milan* (London: Burns and Oates, 1884), 1:76–77.
[8] Ibid., 1:78.

If the lifestyle of the clergy was so blatantly perverse, how could that of the laity differ? So many, just in the city of Milan, had had no contact with the things of God for years. Many who were baptized had never received the other sacraments. Those who had received the Sacrament of Penance and Holy Eucharist had not frequented them for years. Charles often encountered men in their middle to late years who had never been to Confession, while others would think nothing of ten- to fifteen-year absences. There were those who had never been instructed in the most basic Catholic prayers like the Our Father and Hail Mary. Still others had not the slightest idea how to make the sign of the cross, much less to understand what it meant. Things like the Ten Commandments or the precepts of the Church were so foreign as to be almost incomprehensible to many. It goes without saying: if the morals of the clergy were lax, those of the laity were doubly so. Adultery was rampant, and open cohabitation seemed a way of life. Vulgarity even found its way into the city's churches. Local markets would set up commercial operations inside aisles of churches and would transact business and engage in social amenities while the Divine Office was being sung. No wonder the saintly Archbishop would "weep bitterly when on his visits to his diocese he witnessed with his own eyes these miseries".[9]

Despite it all, Charles would not become discouraged. Rather, he would "allow no rest to his body, and grudge ... no labor or fatigue in caring for the salvation of souls".[10] A man of such intense spirituality could not give way to pessimism. Pope Gregory XIV called him the "second Ambrose of Milan", in imitation of the city's fourth-century

[9] Ibid., 1:80.
[10] Ibid., 1:82.

bishop who was renowned for his learning and holiness of life. In fact, Charles had chosen the feast of Saint Ambrose, December 7, 1563, for his consecration as bishop. He always kept a picture of Saint Ambrose near him to inspire him in his work for the salvation of souls. He also had particularly strong attachment to a portrait of Saint John Fisher, the martyred Bishop of Rochester, England, whose commitment to principle in the face of Henry VIII's "reform" made him a defender of the faith whom Charles chose to emulate.

The Archbishop had to become close to his priests and to try to make them holy. He would often go to visit priests unannounced, especially in cases where difficulties existed. Once he knew the particular problem of a priest, either through a personal visit or a matter brought to his attention, he never forgot that priest or his specific difficulty. Interestingly in his own selection of candidates for priestly studies, boys from mountain areas and the outlying districts, where vocations were sparse, were especially welcome and sought after. Some of these young men became fine theologians; many returned to their native towns, where they were especially suited to work among those with whom they had been born and raised. Invariably, they became zealous pastors of souls. The training of such men was extremely important; Charles needed priests to sustain the burden of maintaining so many parishes in his vast archdiocese. He also needed holy men to go into parishes that had been vacant for years; where priests' formation had been poor, he needed specific remedies to strengthen their spirituality and fill in the vacuum in their theological education. Seminaries were to be the answer.

The major archdiocesan seminary was placed under the patronage of Saint John the Baptist, enrolling 150 students at its inception. These were promising young men who would pursue the normal courses of philosophy and theology. A second seminary, the Canonica, was begun for students who had advanced to the study of Scripture, moral theology, and, most importantly, the Roman Catechism. These courses were also given in the third seminary Saint Charles opened, but were meant to be refresher courses for those priests whose training had been deficient. The fervor with which Milan's archbishop approached his task was not lost on many idealistic young men of the day. In fact, his influence was so strong that three additional seminaries had to be opened at various locales within the archdiocese. Charles had always had great esteem for the Jesuits, so he placed his seminaries under their direction, along with several administrative offices in his diocese. By mutual agreement, seminary management eventually was transferred to the Oblates of Saint Ambrose, a community of diocesan priests Charles had begun, who took the simple vow of obedience, serving in various capacities at the Bishop's good pleasure.

In addition, Charles was personally involved in many aspects of priestly formation. Because of his strong belief in a priest's personal holiness, he stressed spiritual development far more than the life of the intellect. Each new candidate was kept separate for a time from the rest of the community and placed under the guidance of a confessor to discern ever more carefully if this was the vocation to which he was called. The Archbishop met personally with each seminarian and kept a file of very detailed notes tracing a man's spiritual progress. Particularly scrutinized before his appointment was the seminary's spiritual director. Charles insisted he be a man well experienced in his field, adept at the practice of mental prayer and examination of conscience. Also, since preaching was one of the principal ways a priest taught and defended the faith, great stress was placed on Sacred Eloquence.

Students were given frequent practice sessions, generally during meal times in the refectory.

Life in Milan's major seminary, the Canonica, has been compared to life in a Capuchin monastery: each seminarian had his own room or cell, over the door of which appeared the Latin word *Asceterium*, indicating it was a place of prayer and meditation. The Archbishop's visits to the seminary "were made with such thoroughness as well as punctuality, that they always lasted a fortnight, during which he never suffered himself to be disturbed by any other business".[11]

Charles was not less stringent in the reforms he carried out to benefit the laity. The Confraternity of Catholic Doctrine was strongly established in the parishes, censors were appointed to examine published books, printers could not issue new books without seeking permission from the "Father Inquisitor", and a supervisory commission called the Index was begun to oversee all literature that might have heretical content. Furthermore,

> all persons belonging to the diocese were forbidden to visit heretical countries, or to hold intercourse with them without express leave in writing, commending the bearer to the especial care of his parish priest.[12]

Finally, Charles required those teaching young people, in whatever capacity, "to make a public profession of their faith, and to preserve their charges from contagion by making use only of approved books".[13]

Such are some of the many ways reform was undertaken in Milan and the integrity of the Catholic faith preserved.

[11] Ibid., 1:113.
[12] Ibid., 1:119–20.
[13] Ibid., 1:120.

All was by no means success for Charles; one religious order in his diocese, called the Humiliati, was anything but humble. The order was decimated, and most of its remaining members were leading degenerate lives. Because they owned large amounts of property and many valuable possessions, they fought vigorously against every reform Charles wanted to enact. Opposition became so pronounced that some of the degenerate clerics contrived a plot to kill the Archbishop; one evening while he was in his chapel saying Evening Prayer, a shot was fired at him:

> St Charles, imagining himself mortally wounded, commended himself to God. But it was found that the bullet had only struck his clothes in the back, raising a bruise, and fallen harmlessly to the floor. After a solemn thanksgiving and procession, he shut himself up for some days in a Carthusian monastery to consecrate his life anew to God.[14]

That was 1569. This holy man, who truly lived the material poverty he so often preached, would survive until 1584. Today, pilgrims from all over the world when visiting the famous Milan Duomo (cathedral) may see his tomb, just a level above the spot where his predecessor Saint Ambrose baptized Saint Augustine. Charles was only forty-six years of age at his death, but what great reform and renewal he activated in his vast archdiocese.

[14] Thurston and Attwater, *Butler's Lives of the Saints*, 4:260.

VI

Martyr of the Reformation:
Thomas More

In his cell in the Tower of London, Thomas More composed his *Dialogue of Comfort against Tribulation*, a work that greatly influenced the later spiritual writing of Saint Francis de Sales. Anyone's spirituality would be profoundly affected by being in More's cell, which can still be visited today by a pilgrim to Catholic London. It is not the cell, of course, but the saint who occupied it that gives the room such an aura of sanctity. Of all who lost their lives at the Reformation, Thomas More is by far the best known and revered. The story of the "man for all seasons" has been told countless times to prove many different points. As a defender of the faith, his life and his death speak clearly and unambiguously.

He was born on February 6, 1478. His parents, John and Agnes Graunger More, sent their young son to Saint Anthony's School on Threadneedle Street in London. The elder More was a lawyer and later a judge; placing great value on the faith, he sent his son to live in the house of the Archbishop of Canterbury. Archbishop Morton saw the young man's academic potential and was instrumental in his going to Oxford. After two years of university life, he entered Lincoln's Inn as a law student and in 1501 was admitted to the bar. Within three years he was a member of Parliament. It was during these events in More's life that he began a life-long friendship with Erasmus of Rotterdam, the famous humanist, scholar, theologian, and satirist.

More was very religious, perhaps from his years under the Archbishop's tutelage, perhaps from his own inclinations. He was very attracted to the London Carthusians, and there is some evidence to suggest the Franciscans had appeal to him. In the end, he chose marriage with Jane Colt of Netherhall in Essex. They were married in 1505 and became the parents of four children: Margaret, Elizabeth, Cecilia, and John, of whom his eldest, Margaret, or Meg, was known to be his most beloved.

More was a brilliantly educated man of the world in the best sense and, without living a monastic life, might be described as an ascetic. He wore a hair shirt, undertook voluntary fasts and penances, assisted at Mass daily, and read portions of the Divine Office. Monsignor Ronald Knox once observed that More was a man who took the best from the Renaissance world, but, in contrast to many of his contemporaries, retained the best of Catholicism. Writing to the Bishop of Vienna in late 1532, Erasmus paints a vivid picture of life in the More household:

> More had built for himself on the banks of the Thames not far from London a country house that is dignified and adequate without being so magnificent as to excite envy. Here he lives happily with his family, consisting of his wife, his son and daughter-in-law, three daughters with their husbands and already eleven grandchildren. It would be difficult to find a man more fond of children than he.... You would say that Plato's Academy had come to life again. But I wrong More's home in comparing it to Plato's Academy, for in the latter the chief subjects of discussion were arithmetic,

geometry and occasionally ethics, but the former rather de-
served the name of a school for the knowledge and practise
of the Christian faith.[1]

The home Erasmus describes is the present-day site of Allen
Hall, the theologate for the archdiocese of Westminster (interestingly, a large oak tree still standing is purported to have
been in place in More's time). In the home, night prayers
were recited by the entire household, including the servants.
At mealtime, one of the More children would read several
verses of Scripture, along with a brief accompanying com-
mentary. More himself seems to have been spiritually nourished by *The Imitation of Christ* by Thomas a Kempis; the
Meditationes Vitae Christi, in his time attributed to Saint
Bonaventure; and the *Scale of Perfection* by the English mystical writer Walter Hilton. In the Borough of Chelsea, not
far from the More estate, one may still visit the chapel Thomas endowed in the parish church, where he regularly sang
in the choir. Chelsea Old Church has been the scene for
several years of the annual Thomas More Lecture, which was
given primarily by Anglicans, highly positive in tone, and
strongly expressive of admiration for many of More's principles and qualities.

The accession of Henry VIII to the throne in 1509 at first
augured well for the young lawyer. Within a year he was
appointed undersheriff of the city of London. His career
seemed to be soaring when tragedy struck. His beloved wife,
Lady Jane, died. Within seven weeks he married Alice Middleton, a widow seven years older than himself. Lady Alice

[1] Erasmus to John Faber, cited in James Monti, *The King's Good Servant but God's First: The Life and Writings of St. Thomas More* (San Francisco: lgnatius Press, 1997), 57.

filled a tremendous gap in the More household. A woman of great common sense, blessed with keen humor and easy conversation, she complemented Master More and brought a great deal of needed love and warmth to the family.

In 1516 More completed *Utopia*, the work for which he is best remembered. In the same year, Henry VIII and his Lord Chancellor, Cardinal Wolsey, determined that More's talents could best be used by active service to the Crown. Thomas did not refuse the many promotions coming his way, but was far more disposed to the scholarly, intellectual life and would have been quite content to remain in such a circumstance. In 1529 he was named Lord Chancellor to succeed Wolsey. To listen to Erasmus, the choice could not have been wiser: "In serious matters no man's advice is more prized, while if the king wishes to recreate himself, no man's conversation is gayer." [2]

More, on the other hand, had no illusions about it all, especially Henry VIII, and he confided to his son-in-law William Roper, "I have no cause to be proud thereof, for if my head would win him a castle in France, it should not fail to go." [3]

One of the more curious notes of history is that Henry VIII had been named Defender of the Faith for an apologetical work in which he strongly defended the office of the papacy. It is even more curious that it appeared at a time when Thomas More's thinking had not developed as fully on the subject. As the years went by, Henry grew more and more frustrated as his queen, Catherine of Aragon, was not producing any male heirs to the throne. He wished to

[2] Cited in Herbert Thurston, S.J., and Donald Attwater, eds., *Butler's Lives of the Saints* (Westminster, Md.: Christian Classics, 1988), 3:51.
[3] Ibid.

divorce her and marry Ann Boleyn, but Pope Clement VII refused to annul the marriage. Such were the beginnings that led to his separation from Rome. Henry imposed on all the clergy an acknowledgment of himself as "Protector and Supreme Head of the Church of England". Initially, the clergy themselves did manage to qualify Henry's title by adding "so far as the law of Christ allows". More wanted to resign his office of Chancellor at this time, but was persuaded to remain to give his attention to what became known at court as the King's "great matter", namely, the granting of a declaration of nullity for his marriage.

This was not to happen. In May 1532, More resigned as Lord Chancellor and the English bishops submitted their loyalty and obedience to Henry as head of the Church of England:

> It is a date as good as any to mark the transition of England from the Middle Ages to modernity. The ancient liberties of the church—liberties that traditionalists claimed came as the gift of Christ Himself—were stripped away. The *Submission of the clergy* is a short document that makes three large concessions: the clergy would never again put forward any law in Convocation without royal consent; Convocation would not meet unless Henry first gave his permission; all the laws of the church were to be reviewed by a joint committee of clergy and laymen. Sixteen ... were to be from Parliament.... Sixteen were to be priests; all thirty two were to be appointed by the king.... On the day after the clergy submitted, Thomas More met the King in the garden of York Palace near Westminster Hall about three in the afternoon, and delivered up the Great Seal.[4]

---

[4] Richard Marius, *Thomas More* (London: Weidenfeld and Nicholson, 1993), 415.

More's resignation did not reduce him to abject poverty, but significantly reduced his income. Many of his household staff were dismissed, and his explanation to his family had to be as positive as the situation would allow:

> [T]hen may we yet with bags and wallets go a-begging together, and hoping that for pity some good folk will give us their charity, at every man's door to sing, '*Salve Regina*', and so still keep company and be merry together.[5]

There is a scene in the movie *A Man for All Seasons*, at Henry's marriage to Anne Boleyn, where the monarch is certain he sees Thomas from the back, only to discover mistaken identity. The scene is substantially correct; More refused to attend. For the next year and a half he quietly busied himself in writing.

On March 23, 1534, Pope Clement VII declared that the marriage of Henry and Catherine of Aragon had indeed been valid. It made little difference to Henry because one week later, on March 30, Parliament passed the Act of Succession, opposition to which constituted high treason. The Act granted legitimate succession to the throne to the offspring of Henry and Anne Boleyn and negated the same to any children of Henry and Catherine. Shortly hereafter, Parliament passed the Act of Supremacy, confirming Henry as Supreme head of the Church of England. With the Acts of Supremacy and Succession accomplished facts, Henry felt himself in an advantageous position. The bishops, with the sole exception of John Fisher, had submitted. More had resigned, and the country was in great confusion. All seemed to be going according to the monarch's plan. In particular, he felt the Act of Supremacy very successful since it

---

[5] Thurston and Attwater, *Butler's Lives of the Saints*, 3:52.

ended the papal jurisdiction in England, although clearly Henry would accept that jurisdiction if the pope would only rule in favor of his divorce. The ecclesiastical theory behind the act was that the church was inspired in the whole body by the Holy Spirit and that the pope was unnecessary to the unity of Catholic doctrine, that indeed he was an obstacle to the inspiration that made the church of one mind in all places where Christians might dwell.[6]

There was one potential obstacle: Could Thomas More present any sort of problem to Henry by his actions?

Englishmen knew their history, and to any historical-minded person, Thomas More represented a clear and present danger to the revolution Henry was making, a mortal threat to Henry's throne and to Henry's life. By refusing to attend the coronation ... Thomas More was quietly raising a flag. It did not require much imagination to see it fluttering softly in its place on a hill apart, waiting for other men like himself to rally around it.[7]

More was not consciously orchestrating this, though he likely knew people paid a great deal of attention to his words and actions:

He shrank from martyrdom, but if martyrdom should come, his church would have the benefit of his example, heightened by meek innocence, which would make the character of the tyrant all the more stark and terrible.[8]

The great majority of Catholics in England did not follow Thomas More's example. True, many of the northern Cath-

---

[6] Marius, *Thomas More*, 432.
[7] Ibid., 442.
[8] Ibid.

olic families who came to be known as recusants were left alone if they remained silent and docile; still, most took the Oath of Supremacy, often adding the reservation "so long as it not be contrary to the law of God". On April 13, 1534, More and John Fisher, Bishop of Rochester, were tendered the Oath and both refused. More was placed in the custody of the Abbot of Westminster Abbey and twice more refused. For this he was incarcerated in the Tower of London for fifteen months. It was to be a time of prayer, meditation, spiritual writing, and growth in holiness. During this time his family tried, to no avail, to see if there were any way his conscience would allow him to take the Oath. As time wore on, visits with family members became less and less frequent, then ceased altogether. One relationship that grew deeper was that with his daughter Meg, through visits and correspondence. William Roper, Meg's husband, cites a particularly poignant passage from one of More's letters: "I find no cause, I thank God, Meg, to reckon myself in worse case here than at home, for methinks God maketh me a wanton and setteth me on His lap and dandleth me." [9]

On February 1, 1535, the Act of Supremacy officially recognized Henry's ecclesiastical headship in England, became law, and made any denial of the same a treasonable offense. Thomas Cromwell, the King's principal secretary, paid a visit to Thomas and asked his opinion of the bill, but he would not give one. The months passed quickly, and in May he and his daughter Meg were to have their final visit. During that visit, the two watched a memorable event from the window of More's cell. Carthusians from the Charterhouse in London had joined More and Fisher in their refusal to recognize

---

[9] Thurston and Attwater, *Butler's Lives of the Saints*, 3:53.

Henry's claim. On this particular day, several of those holy men went to their death:

> Lo! doest thou not see, Meg, that these blessed fathers be now as cheerfully going to their deaths as bridegrooms to their marriage? . . . Whereas thy silly father, Meg, that like a most wicked caitiff hath passed forth the whole course of his miserable life most sinfully, God thinking him not so worthy so soon to come to that eternal felicity, leaveth him here yet still in the world further to be plagued and turmoiled with misery.[10]

A few days after Meg's visit, Thomas Cromwell came to the Tower once more to solicit More's views concerning the Act of Supremacy, but he was unsuccessful. More declared: "I have not been a man of such holy living as I might be bold to offer myself to death, lest God for my presumption might suffer me to fall."[11]

On June 19, 1535, three more Carthusians suffered martyrdom on Tower Hill, and on the twenty-second, John Fisher was beheaded. It was the feast of Saint Alban, Protomartyr of Britain, though in recent times More and Fisher have been assigned this feast.

Nine days after John Fisher's death, More was indicted and tried for treason in Westminster Hall. The television portrait of a sickly man seated is indeed accurate. He listened as attentively as possible to the charges that his comments in conversations with visitors as well as those with Sir Richard Rich, the solicitor general, were treasonable. More could simply reiterate his silence on the entire issue, while confessing to his jurors:

[10] Ibid.
[11] Ibid.

Ye must understand that, in things touching conscience, every true and good subject is more bound to have respect to his said conscience and to his soul than to any other thing in all the world beside.[12]

He was found guilty and condemned to death.

In the end, More was dying for the principle of papal primacy. It was a notion that grew in him through the years, one to which he gave more and more time, in light of Henry VIII's once firm defense. James Monti, in his work *The King's Good Servant but God's First*, sees the change in More coming in the early 1520s. He cites Cardinal Reginald Pole, the last Catholic Archbishop of Canterbury and an acquaintance of More's, and Spanish Dominican Pedro de Soto, who had spoken with those who had known More well, as attesting that More had explained his position to his close friend Antonio Bonvisi:

> According to Pole, while discussing the growing Protestant schism, More indicated that it was the dissenters' new tenets on the Holy Eucharist that troubled him the most, whereas their attacks on papal primacy seemed to him of lesser concern. No sooner had he said this than he began to have second thoughts, and confessing immediately to Bonvisi that he had spoken thus "without consideration", he asked him to come again to discuss this question. . . . After a fairly short interval—Pole says it was only ten or twelve days, while deSoto says it was about a month—More and his friend met once again, and . . . the former immediately began by reproaching himself. . . . Alas! Mr. Bonvisi, . . . when I made you that answer on the primacy of the Church . . . O my friend, how solid are the grounds on which the primacy of the Roman pontiff rests! In fact, it is not only most firmly

established in the Christian religion but is itself the ground and foundation of all the rest.[13]

More changed his thinking based on his study of sources, though the sources he consulted were never recorded; only the statements of Pole and de Soto attest to it. Apparently what More read sufficiently convinced him that one side was decidedly correct, the other not. That conviction he made quite clear:

> I [have] never neither read nor heard any thing of such effect on the other side, that ever could lead me to think that my conscience were well discharged, but rather in right great peril if I should follow the other side and deny the primacy to be provided by God.[14]

Richard Marius, a More scholar and biographer, explains the mind of Thomas:

> To say that the papacy was a human invention was to say that the papal office was designed by human minds for the convenience of the church, and that those same minds might design some other form of government that might serve just as well. . . . If the papacy had endured as long as it had, God must have set the office in the church, and Christians could not change it on whim.[15]

An even larger question than papal primacy for More was the unity of the Church and how the Church heard the voice of God:

[13] Monti, *The King's Good Servant*, 154.
[14] Elizabeth Rogers, *The Correspondence of Sir Thomas More*, Letter No. 199, cited in Monti, *King's Good Servant*, 154–55.
[15] Marius, *Thomas More*, 457.

A fragment of the Catholic Church, splitting itself away from the whole body, could not hear that voice, for a fragment was not party to the revelations of the whole any more than a severed arm shares in the life of the body it has left behind.[16]

More understood that the primacy or headship of the Pope was the principal source of unity and strength upon which Christ had built his Church, and without that principle the Church could not survive in unified fashion. He was correct, though the majority of his countrymen could not see it at the time. Hilaire Belloc, a Catholic apologist and historian, expressed amazement that More could have had the courage of such convictions:

> He could foresee no fruit following upon his great example. . . . He was absolutely alone. He had nothing within or without, nothing promised in the future, nothing inherited from the past, nothing in the traditions of his habits and life, to nerve him for what he did. And yet he did it.[17]

Early on the morning of July 6, 1535, "the King's good servant but God's first" was informed that he would die that day. At age fifty-seven, his life ended with one stroke and his mortal remains were placed with many others in the church of Saint Peter in Chains, inside the Tower walls. His head remained atop a pole on Tower Bridge, but was finally retrieved by his daughter Meg, who had it placed in the Roper vault in the church of Saint Dunstan, outside the west gate of the city of Canterbury, where devout Christians still go in prayer.

[16] Ibid., 458.
[17] Hilaire Belloc, *Characters of the Reformation* (Rockford, Ill.: Tan Books and Publishers, 1992), 63.

More was beatified with other English martyrs in 1886 and canonized a saint of the Church in 1935. Five years later, Monsignor Ronald Knox found great significance in the timing of his long overdue canonization:

> Times like these, do not let us deceive ourselves about it, are difficult to live in for a Catholic who loves his faith. There is a continual apparent contrast between the restless speculations of the modern intellect, and those abiding certainties by which we live. The question continually arises: Is such and such a view, which I see propounded in the newspapers, consistent with Catholic truth? Is such and such a political expedient, which I see prominent men are advocating, justifiable in the light of Catholic doctrine? We are hurried along breathlessly by the spirit of the age in which we live, yet protesting all the time, questioning all the time. . . .
>
> In such times, let us thank God's mercy for giving us the example and the protection of a great Saint, our own fellow-countryman, who knew how to absorb all that was best in the restless culture of his day, yet knew at once, when the time came, that he must make a stand here; that he must give no quarter to the modern world here.[18]

Over six decades later, might not this defender of the faith have words to speak to our world as well?

[18] Ronald Knox, *Captive Flames* (London: Burns and Oates, 1940), 79–80.

VII

John Fisher: Bishop of Rochester

The city of Rochester, England, is similar to many other cities in Britain, where centuries-old buildings exist side by side with modern structures. The Cathedral of Rochester is one such building of antiquity; just inside its main door is a commemorative plaque honoring all of the former bishops of the diocese. Aside from the listing of John Fisher's name, precious few, if any, memories survive of the great defender of the faith who headed the see in the sixteenth century.

Fisher was a native Yorkshireman born in 1469. At fourteen he was enrolled in Cambridge University, a significant academic accomplishment. At twenty-two (with special permission) he was ordained to the priesthood, an even greater spiritual accomplishment. Throughout his life, Rochester's future bishop (he was appointed to the see at age thirty-five) would combine profound scholarship with conspicuous holiness. At Cambridge he became senior proctor, master of Michaelhouse (which later became Trinity College), and Vice-Chancellor of the university and also received the degree of Doctor of Divinity. With each position came greater responsibility and an opportunity to make necessary improvements:

> When he went to Cambridge, its scholarship had sunk to a
> low ebb: no Greek or Hebrew was taught, and the library

had been reduced to 300 volumes.... [H]e did much, entirely on his own initiative, to foster learning at the university. He endowed scholarships, he re-introduced Greek and
Hebrew into the curriculum, and he brought Erasmus over
to teach and to lecture.[1]

It was no surprise when Fisher became the university's Chancellor. But, it may well have surprised Fisher, however, when
he was asked to assume the duties of Bishop of Rochester.
Nonetheless, he saw God's will and became a shepherd of
enormous pastoral sensitivity. The poor, the sick, and the
dying were all objects of his personal concern. When a priest
of his diocese was experiencing difficulties, he often intervened, and if discipline was called for, he did not refrain from
doing what had to be done. He could often be seen in the
city's streets distributing alms. Amid all this, Fisher kept up
an extensive writing, lecturing, and speaking career.

The Bishop was austere in his lifestyle and devoid of any
personal ambition. He was never given to overindulgence,
and while eating, he had the unusual habit of keeping a human skull on the table as a reminder of death. If he found
any earthly pleasure, it would be in his books; he built up
one of the finest libraries in Europe, fully intending to be-
queath it to Cambridge. The personal holiness he tried to
cultivate was one he wanted to share with his brother priests.
He had no desire to climb the ecclesiastical ladder (he turned
down several offers to assume larger dioceses) and felt strongly
that the sort of lives priests led affected their own salvation
and that of others. In 1518, Cardinal Wolsey called a synod
of the clergy, at which Fisher, quoting Cardinal Wolsey, spoke:

[1] Herbert Thurston, S.J., and Donald Attwater, eds., *Butler's Lives of the
Saints* (Westminster, Md.: Christian Classics, 1988), 3:46.

'For what should we' [said Cardinal Wolsey] 'exhort our flocks to eschew and shun worldly ambition, when we ourselves that be bishops do wholely set our minds to the same things we forbid in them? What example of Christ our Saviour do we imitate, who first exercised doing and after fell to teaching? If we teach according to our doing, how absurd may our doctrine be accounted? If we teach one thing and do another, our labour in teaching shall never benefit our flock half so much as our examples in doing shall hurt them.' [2]

How Fisher felt the lives of the clergy affected those of the flock entrusted to them has been studied by E. E. Reynolds, one of his biographers:

He recognized two weaknesses in the state of the Church; few priests and even few bishops, were theologians or had a sound grounding in the "queen of sciences". There had also been a decline in the art and practice of preaching and teaching amongst the secular clergy. In far too many parishes there was need for careful instruction in the faith. It was these ordinary parishioners that John Fisher had in mind; he was not thinking of academic scholarship as an end in itself, but he had hoped that, gradually, the secular clergy would be more fitted for their high calling. [3]

His was always a pastoral vocation. William Rastell, a young contemporary, sums up both these aspects, as it were, in a laudatory way:

He was in holiness, learning and diligence in his cure and in his fulfilling his office of bishop such that of many hundred years England had not any bishop worthy to be compared

[2] E. E. Reynolds, *Saint John Fisher* (New York: P. J. Kenedy and Sons, 1955), 57–58.
[3] Ibid., 15.

unto him. And if all countries of Christendom were searched, there could not lightly among all other nations be found one that hath been in all things like unto him, so well used and fulfilled the office of bishop as he did. He was of such high perfection in holy life and strait and austere living as few were, I suppose, in all Christendom in his time, religious or other.[4]

This bishop of exemplary holiness and pastoral sensitivity was also a recognized theologian. As such, he was called on to defend the truths of faith against many heretical teachings prevalent in his time. Heresy had not been a serious problem in England prior to the coming of John Wycliff. In his reformed theology, Wycliff took the idea of equality before God too far. If all were equal, he felt, how could those ordained (bishops and priests) lay claim to any special status? Each person could atone for his own sins and did not need the mediation of anyone else. Further, if a bishop's or priest's personal life was not completely beyond reproach (and many were not), this merely enhanced Wycliff's argument. An organized church might be a help to people's spiritual lives, but it was not a necessity. If it were to continue existing and hope to accomplish anything, it must rid itself of hierarchical trappings, ornate liturgy, and the like.

Once the British door of receptivity had been opened to Wycliff, it was easier for other reformers to advance their views. They did, in rapid succession, until the major influx of Lutheran books and tracts in 1520. They became a cause of great concern to the Catholic bishops of England. Individuals found with heretical books in their possession could be brought before ecclesiastical magistrates, though few cases

---

[4] Nicholas Harpsfield, E. W. Hitchcock and R. W. Chambers, eds., *The Life and Death of Sir Thomas More* (1932), 249, cited in Reynolds, *Saint John Fisher*, 59–60.

were ever reported. In May 1521, Cardinal Wolsey declared a public burning of all heretical books in England, a response, in part, to *Exsurge Domine*, a papal bull of a year earlier condemning over forty of Luther's propositions. Fisher preached on this occasion, assuring his hearers of the Holy Spirit's constant assistance in protecting the teaching Church from error:

> [T]he Holy Spirit which is the third person in the divinity was sent from the father Almighty God and from his son, our saviour Christ Jesu, to be the spirit of truth residing for ever in the church of Christ, and to be as a comforter from time to time against all storms and tempests of heresies ascertaining us in the time of every doubtfulness the very truth whereunto we shall hold and keep us.[5]

The Bishop supported his arguments by quoting from the Scriptures and the Fathers, "but the sermon was not overloaded with scholarship; it was not John Fisher's custom to parade his learning; it was the solid foundation on which he based his preaching."[6]

Meanwhile, in reply to the Pope's condemnation of his forty-two propositions, Luther wrote his *Assertio*, published near the end of 1520. In January 1523, John Fisher's reply to Luther, the *Confutatio*, was published at Antwerp, Belgium. Over the next thirteen years, Fisher's highly theological response was reprinted many times, both in English and German. It singled him out in his own day as a real defender of the faith. On the back of the book's title page are some Latin verses written by George Daye, one of John Fisher's chaplains at Cambridge. These translate as follows:

[5] Ibid., 89.
[6] Ibid., 90.

This is the pugilist of Christ,
Shining with uprightness of life,
Renowned in genius and eloquence,
Whom England nourished and Cambridge taught
Rochester holds, ennobled by such a man.[7]

The four volumes Fisher wrote against Luther constitute the first scholarly refutation of the "new doctrines". Tremendous service to the Church that it was, the Bishop of Rochester never took personal pride in it. He confided to a fellow cleric that if he could bring back all the hours spent in research and writing, they would have been far better spent in personal prayer.

Ultimately, the saintly Bishop would be called on to defend the faith not merely by his writing and preaching but with his life. The issue, as with Saint Thomas More, involved the question of King Henry VIII's marriage to Catherine of Aragon, who had not given him the male heir he so desperately wanted. Further, as a man given totally to depraved carnal desires, Henry's passion for Anne Boleyn was also a strong motivator in his attempts to divorce the Queen. He hoped for a declaration of nullity based on the fact that Catherine had been married to his deceased brother. Henry's "argument" was taken from Leviticus 20:21 and his reading of the illegitimacy of such an action. The fact that Catherine was indeed a widow when she and Henry married does not seem to have played a part in his thinking. John Fisher was strongly of the opinion that the Pope had the right to grant a dispensation allowing Henry to marry Catherine and there was no way the marriage could be considered anything but valid. Early in the summer of 1527,

[7] Ibid., 92.

Wolsey informed the monarch of Fisher's opinion. He felt, quite correctly, that Henry would be displeased. After a few months the King decided the best course of action was to meet with the Bishop to discuss the matter personally. It was a courteous, if not outwardly friendly, meeting, in which Fisher assured Henry his marriage to Catherine had indeed been lawful. For Fisher, it was the beginning of the end:

> These and divers like words he there uttered to the king, which might have satisfied his sick mind had he not been otherwise perversely bent, and therefore all was in vain.... And so for that time my Lord of Rochester departed from the king who from that date forward never looked on him with merry countenance as the good bishop did well perceive for that his grudge daily increased towards him.[8]

Henry's grudge would have even more reason to increase when Bishop Fisher was chosen to be one of the Queen's counselors in the nullity suit, which was heard by Cardinal Campeggio at Blackfriars, the Dominican residence at Oxford. Delivering his opinion, the Bishop could not have been more forceful in defending the Church and the papacy. The arguments he used to uphold the validity of the marriage bond were scholarly and precise, although he did insert an appeal equally emotional, noting that John the Baptist had died for the same principle. Henry was said to have become livid, and though Fisher's direct contact with the case ceased, he had made many enemies and his future was in jeopardy.

Proof of this came on one occasion when food poisoning was discovered in soup served in the Bishop's home. Two servants died; scores became violently ill. Thankfully the

[8] Fr. Van Ortroy, S.J., ed., *Vie du bienheureux martyr Jean Fisher*, Bollandist (Brussels, 1893), 176–79, cited in Reynolds, *Saint John Fisher*, 138.

Bishop managed to avoid eating any of it, but sometime later another episode occurred:

> Suddenly a gun was shot through the top of his house, not far from his study where he accustomably used to sit. Which made such a terrible noise over his head and bruised the tiles and rafters of the house so sore, that both he and divers others of his servants were suddenly amazed thereat. Wherefore, speedy search was made whence this shot should come and what it meant. Which at last was found to come from the other side of the Thames, out of the Earl of Wiltshire's house, who was father to the Lady Anne.[9]

Whether Anne Boleyn and her relatives were responsible for the shooting is a matter for conjecture. One thing, though, is certain: "The Lady fears no one here more than the Bishop of Rochester, for it is he who has always defended the queen's cause."[10]

From this point on, the fate of John Fisher follows closely that of Thomas More. Both were commanded to take the Oath of Supremacy, declaring Henry supreme head of the Church of England. Both refused. John Fisher was summoned to appear at Lambeth on April 13, 1534, to take the Oath that was required by the Act of Succession. The other bishops and members of the House of Lords had taken it at the end of the Parliamentary session. Specifically, he appeared (on the same day as More) before a commission consisting of Thomas Cranmer, Archbishop of Canterbury; Sir Thomas Audley, Lord Chancellor; Thomas Cromwell, the King's secretary; and William Benson, Abbott of Westminster. Fisher asked to see the Oath and for time to think it

---

[9] Ortroy, *Vie*, 226, cited in Reynolds, *Saint John Fisher*, 181.
[10] Ibid.

over. The commissioners agreed and allowed him to return to his own home. On the seventeenth of April, the Oath was again presented to Fisher and to More. Both refused to sign it and were sent to the Tower of London. E. E. Reynolds explains:

> Let us be quite clear why they refused to take the oath. They did not question the power of parliament to determine the succession; that, after all, was in keeping with English tradition; they would have taken an oath that bound them to that and nothing else, but ... far more involved.... To put it briefly, the oath meant acceptance of the repudiation of the Pope's authority implied by the Act, where he is called the "Bishop of Rome". Fisher and More were convinced that the papal primacy was of divine institution, and, therefore, not to be set aside by an earthly authority.... [They] separated the office from the holder of the office. The Petrine powers passed unimpaired from pope to pope, however unworthy might be the human agent. Allied to this ... was the paramount need to maintain the unity of the Church. A leading theme in Fisher's thought was the Church as the Mystical Body of Christ; to separate oneself from it was to him the ultimate betrayal.[11]

John Fisher and Thomas More were kept strictly separated in the Tower, and while both were initially deprived of such items as books, writing materials, and so forth, the overall treatment accorded Fisher appears harsher. He was not allowed the consolation of the sacraments, nor was he permitted to attend Mass in one of the Tower chapels. Henry had an unusual vengeance for Fisher because as the bishop of a diocese Fisher could strongly influence people's opinions and

[11] E. E. Reynolds, *Saint John Fisher*, rev. ed. (Wheathampstead, Hertfordshire: Anthony Clarke Books, 1955, 1972), 226.

strongest emotions through his preaching and writing. Now, weakened by age and appearing years older than was actually the case, Fisher is described by Cardinal Reginald Pole:

> When I left England three years ago [1532] I thought that even then if he should use the greatest possible care about his health in his own house, considering what he suffered, he could not live another year. And I heard afterwards that when he was summoned to London to be imprisoned, on the journey he swooned away for some time from weakness.[12]

The fact is also borne out by Rowland Lee, Bishop of Coventry and Litchfield and one of those consecrated by Cranmer in 1534 after the break from Rome. Lee, along with many of his Protestant Episcopal confreres, visited Fisher and tried to persuade him to change his mind. All such attempts failed, but in reporting his particular failure to Cromwell, Lee added: "Surely the man is nigh gone and doubtless cannot stand [survive] unless the King and his council be merciful to him, for the body cannot bear the clothes on his back."[13]

In the Calendar of the Letters and Papers . . . of the Reign of Henry the VIII, there are many fragments of the writings of Fisher. Commentaries on the Psalms and pieces on the Eucharist and on the dignity of the clergy all survived, much of it written in Rochester. One particular prayer is believed to have been composed in the Tower or when knowledge of that fate was certain: "Rescue me from these manifold perils

---

[12] Reginald Pole, Pro ecclesiasticae unitatis defensione, book 3, f. cxviv, cited in Reynolds, *Saint John Fisher* (1955), 218.

[13] Calendar of the Letters and Papers . . . of the Reign of Henry the VIII, 7:498, cited in Reynolds, *Saint John Fisher* (1955), 253.

that I am in, for unless thou wilt of thine infinite goodness relieve me, I am but as a lost creature." [14]

He knew well that he shared humanity's need for the mercy of God. He likewise knew that to face what was in store nothing would suffice short of the Holy Spirit, "by whose gracious presence I may be warmed, heated, and kindled with the spiritual fire of charity and with the sweetly burning love of all godly affection". [15]

On May 20, 1535, just one month short of Fisher's death, Pope Paul III startled many in England by naming the saintly Bishop "a Cardinal Priest of the title of Saint Vitalis". The Pope believed such an honor might save the Bishop's life and at the same time improve the relationship between Britain and the Holy See. He was wrong on both counts. Henry's agent in Rome, Sir Gregory Casale, in a private audience with the Holy Father strongly protested the action as an insult to his king. As for government reaction, it is well summed up in Henry's own comment: "Well, let the pope send him a hat, when he will. But I will so provide that, whensoever it cometh, he shall wear it on his shoulders, for head shall he have none to see it on." [16]

The results of the Bishop's trial, never in doubt, were made public June 17, 1534. He was to be hanged, drawn, and quartered. However, probably fearing that Fisher would die on the way to Tyburn, the king changed the sentence to beheading. This sentence was carried out on a plain near the Tower of London five days later, and a remarkable testimony

[14] *Letters and Papers*, VIII, no. 887, cited in Reynolds, *Saint John Fisher* (1955), 252.

[15] Reynolds, *Saint John Fisher* (1955), 252.

[16] Ortroy, *Vie*, 311, cited in Reynolds, *Saint John Fisher* (1955), 264. See also Thurston, *Butler's Lives of the Saints*, 3:48.

to the man's spirituality came on the morning of his death: when notified he would die later that morning, he merely asked for a bit more time to rest and slept soundly for two hours, totally at peace with his Creator. After reading the New Testament briefly and offering a prayer for his executioner:

> [w]ith a clear voice he said that he was dying for the faith of Christ's Holy Catholic Church, and he asked the people to pray that he might be steadfast to the end. After he recited the *Te Deum* and the psalm *In te Domine speravi*, he was blind-folded, and with one blow from the axe his head was severed from his body.[17]

The Bishop's mortal remains were literally thrown into a grave near the Tower in as undignified a manner as one could imagine, born of pure hostility. Because so many began coming to the site to pray for and to this holy man, his body was exhumed and placed with so many others in the church of Saint Peter in Chains inside the Tower. His head and those of the Carthusians who preceded him in death were placed on the Tower Bridge and Fisher's was only removed to make room for Thomas More's.

The cause of the English Martyrs gained tremendous momentum with the restoration of the hierarchy in 1850, though more than three decades would pass before Pope Leo XIII officially recognized "the honour given to the Blessed Martyrs John Cardinal Fisher, Thomas More and others put to death in England for the Faith from the year 1535 to 1583".[18]

With the four hundredth anniversary of their deaths approaching in 1935, many again hoped to see them canon-

---

[17] Thurston and Attwater, *Butler's Lives of the Saints*, 3:48.
[18] Reynolds, *Saint John Fisher* (1955), 294.

ized, and their hopes were fulfilled on the nineteenth of May of that year. Five years earlier, the cause had been formally opened and the investigation begun. Pope Pius XI granted a dispensation from the usual proof of miracles necessary for canonization and the statesman and bishop were both raised to the altars of sainthood. Reginald Pole, the last Catholic Archbishop of Canterbury, stated well the spirituality of John Fisher. In 1935 his words were particularly insightful. Through the decades their poignancy became even more pronounced:

> What other have you, or have you had for centuries, to compare with Rochester in holiness, in learning, in prudence and in episcopal zeal? You may be, indeed, proud of him, for, were you to search through all the nations in Christendom in our days, you would not easily find one who was such a model of episcopal virtues.[19]

---

[19] Ibid., 295.

VIII

Edmund Campion: the Seditious Jesuit

The English Jesuit Edmund Campion, son of a London bookseller, was born in 1540. He lived most of his adult life during the reign of Queen Elizabeth I (1558–1603). It was a very difficult time for Catholics in England. Elizabeth, the daughter of Henry VIII and Anne Boleyn, was Queen Mary Tudor's half sister and had succeeded her on the throne after her death. Elizabeth restored and further Protestantized the Church of England that her father had begun, and though she was now the official head of the church,

> she was certainly not a religious woman; she was ... resolved to restore Royal supremacy over the English church. A sovereign who, addressing Parliament, threatened to depose her Bishops if they did not carry out her wishes, was not the woman to accept the supremacy of the Pope. A Puritan critic remarked that the only doctrine on which she insisted was that of Royal supremacy.[1]

---

[1] E. I. Watkin, *Roman Catholicism in England from the Reformation to 1950* (London: Oxford University Press, 1957), 15.

An earlier biographer of Edmund Campion is even more to the point in her description of life in Elizabethan England:

> Religion in itself troubled the Court party as little as anything could possibly do. It was because the spirit of Catholicism seemed to them to threaten their particular kind of national pride, and to interfere with their particular kind of worldly prosperity, that they tried to put it down. They wished to get good citizenship acknowledged not as an ideal, but as the supreme ideal, and they cared not how much else was shoveled out of the way. Their only use for religion was to bring it well under the authority of the law and the supremacy of the Crown.[2]

Edmund Campion's family had been Catholic until the reign of Elizabeth I, but they conformed to the established church sometime after 1558. The younger Campion was a brilliant student and a skilled orator. At the age of fifteen he had entered Saint John's College at Oxford and within two years became a Junior Fellow. It was not difficult for him to be noticed at court, especially after being chosen to give an oration at Oxford in the Queen's presence. A member of her court was quick to describe Campion as "one of the diamonds of England"[3], and a bishop friend persuaded him, upon finishing his education, to take orders in the Church of England. He did, but amid great hesitancy. During his undergraduate years he had become a serious student of the Fathers of the Church, and the more he studied them, the more difficult it became for him to accept the validity of the Church of England.

---

[2] Louise Imogen Guiney, *Blessed Edmund Campion* (London: R. and T. Washbourne, 1914), 9–10.

[3] Herbert Thurston, S.J., and Donald Attwater, eds., *Butler's Lives of the Saints* (Westminster, Md.: Christian Classics, 1988), 4:466.

Campion became a junior proctor at Oxford in 1568; upon completion of his teaching duties in 1569, he decided to leave for Ireland to sort out his thinking. He seemed to be growing restless and very remorseful about being in a church in which he felt the fullness of truth was not found. Campion was not one to keep quiet about his misgivings, making many aware of his feelings. When Pope Saint Pius V issued a Bull of Deposition against Queen Elizabeth, the future saint immediately became a suspect in his native land. He returned from Ireland for a brief visit in 1576 and is said to have been present in Westminster Hall, London, for the trial of a convicted papist. He knew he had to leave England, but experienced considerable difficulty getting out of the country without a proper passport. Only by giving up his personal belongings could he escape. When he returned, it would be as a very changed man.

Campion made his way to the town of Douai in Belgium, then part of the Spanish Netherlands. The University of Douai had been established in 1559 by Phillip II of Spain to promote the Counter-Reformation. It flourished into a great center of learning and became an ideal academic setting for English exiles who could no longer hope for Catholic higher education in their native land. The dream of opening an English college had long been cherished by William Allen, a Lancashireman and a future cardinal of the Church. Coming from a staunch Catholic family in the north of England, Allen had a deep concern for his coreligionists who were forced to attend Mass clandestinely and to attend Anglican services for fear of being fined if they refused to do so. Those who did refuse became known as recusants. Allen was determined to better the recusants' lot by providing them a well-educated native clergy. Following his priestly ordination at Malines, Belgium, in 1568, he opened the English college at Douai:

[His] intention was to foster a collegiate life similar to that at Oxford, preparing Catholic scholars for that day when England would return to the Catholic fold. However, as it grew increasingly unlikely that this cherished dream would be achieved, at least not without the intervention of some foreign power, it became obvious to Allen and his collaborators, that the provision for a well-trained Catholic clergy for work in England was an urgent necessity.[4]

The English priests educated at Douai would return to find a flock widely dispersed, low in morale, and greatly in need of spiritual teaching and encouragement. Such men had to be well trained in theology, philosophy, Scripture, and, particularly, apologetics. They had to know the faith thoroughly in order to engage in debate with all sorts of heretical adversaries. The young men who entered the English college were on fire with the needed spiritual enthusiasm, and among their number the eighteenth arrival was Edmund Campion.

It is not exactly clear when Campion formally made his profession of faith and reconciled with the Church of Rome; perhaps it was in London, or perhaps upon arrival in Douai. In any event, he took his Bachelor of Divinity degree at the university in 1573 and was ordained a subdeacon. Shortly thereafter, something happened:

He told Dr. Allen he wished to leave his present life, go on pilgrimage, in the spirit of penance, to the tomb of the Apostles at Rome, and there seek admission into the Society of Jesus. The medieval Orders would have less attraction for Campion: he was an intensely "modern" man. Now this was a severe blow to Allen: hardly less so to others of Campion's

---

[4] Stewart Foster, O.S.M., *Cardinal William Allen: 1532–1594* (London: Catholic Truth Society, 1993), 4.

circle. Campion, the pride, the example, the hope of the
seminary, to quit it for good, and to quit it in order to join
the most recent of religious communities—one which as yet
had few English members! It was inexplicable. But Allen,
like the greathearted and broad-minded commander-in-
chief he was, let him go without protest. He little foresaw
that far from losing his most promising champion, he was
but lending him to better masters of the interior life than
himself, and would receive his trained strength again in the
English Mission's spiritual day of battle.[5]

Campion was entering a very new religious foundation in
the Church. Ignatius Loyola had established the Society of
Jesus six years before his birth. There was no English province; the nearest Jesuit house was in Vienna, and after spend-
ing some time there, Campion went to the novitiate in Prague.
Further studies followed, and he was ordained to the priesthood in 1578. The city of Prague that Edmund Campion
knew has been described as being "in a miserable, godless
state; the Catholics were poor and few: the great university
had perished."[6]

A formidable statue of heretic John Hus is to be seen to
this day in Prague's town square. It was his reformed theology, together with that of John Wycliffe and others, that had
so devastated Catholic spiritual life in the fifteenth century.
The more Campion dwelled on this, the more he concluded
his native land was at least partially to blame. Reformed
thought had crossed the channel from England to the Continent; all the more reason to return to England and firmly
plant the seeds of faith.

[5] Guiney, *Blessed Edmund Campion*, 58.
[6] Ibid., 62–63.

It is not surprising that Cardinal Allen would have persuaded Pope Gregory XIII to send Jesuits to England. In places like Germany, Bohemia, and Poland, they had made great strides for the Counter-Reformation. The Society chose Fathers Edmund Campion and Robert Persons to be the first to go to the English mission. Before Campion left Prague an interesting event occurred: "A white-haired Silesian, Father James Gall, wrote in scroll fashion, by night, over the outer door of that same [Campion's] little room: P[ater] Edmundus Campianus, Martyr." [7]

Campion left for England by way of Rome in the spring of 1580:

> When they got to the Protestant stronghold of Geneva Campion pretended to be an Irish serving-man called Patrick, and they all seem to have behaved with that reckless cheerfulness that makes more serious-minded people think the English mad. [8]

One of his companions, Father Persons, had set out from Saint Omer in French Flanders disguised as a soldier. Campion changed his disguise, pretending to be a jewel merchant traveling with his servant, also a disguised Jesuit (a lay brother named Ralph Sherwin). When the three arrived in London, there was a real chance they would be captured. They quickly dispersed; Campion went to the counties of Berkshire, Oxfordshire, and Northamptonshire, where he made a significant number of converts. He returned to London for a brief meeting with Persons, but persecution was so intense that he had to flee again, this time to Lancashire in the north, where he once again experienced great apostolic

[7] Ibid., 73.
[8] Thurston and Attwater, *Butler's Lives of the Saints*, 4:467.

success, even with the threat of capture. He recounted much of this to his Jesuit superiors:

> I ride about some piece of the country every day. The harvest is wonderful great. . . . I cannot long escape the hands of the heretics. . . . I am in apparel to myself very ridiculous; I often change it and my name also. I read letters sometimes myself that, in the first front, tell news that Campion is taken, which roused in every place that I come so filleth my ears with the sound thereof that fear itself hath taken away all fear.[9]

During these years of intense missionary activity, Campion also wrote his *Decem Rationes* (*Ten Reasons*). It was an apologetic work meant to defend Catholic truth, while at the same time engaging Protestants in debate. The difficulty was how to circulate this work throughout England; one publisher had already been hanged at Tyburn for printing Catholic literature, and this could not be allowed to happen again. The answer to this dilemma came from the Stonors, a devout recusant family in Oxfordshire, near Henley, where a famous regatta is held annually.

The Stonor family had been deeply loyal to the British monarchy for generations. Thomas Stonor had been one of the four horsemen who had accompanied the body of King Henry VII at his funeral. Thomas' son, Walter, remained loyal to the crown in all matters save religion, but he was a pragmatic man who felt silence on the issue was the most prudent course for himself and his family. Interestingly, he served his entire adult life as a member of the King's Commission for the Peace in Oxfordshire; its primary purpose was capturing "recusant papists". Upon the death of Walter

---

[9] Cited in Thurston and Attwater, *Butler's Lives of the Saints*, 4:467.

Stonor the care of Stonor Park fell to Francis Stonor, Walter's son; he, too, was content to live quietly. Francis died shortly after the accession of Elizabeth I, and his wife, Lady Cecily, became matriarch of the family's estate and holdings. She was of an entirely different disposition from her husband. A niece of the Carthusian Sebastian Newdigate, who was hanged, drawn, and quartered during the reign of Henry VIII for refusing to renounce his faith, Lady Cecily was determined to do her part in the restoration of Catholicism:

> [She] decamped to Stonor Lodge, and turned the main house into a refuge for a new generation of priests, the product of the seminary at Douai dedicated to turning out the foot soldiers who would win back "Mary's Dowry," England, for the Pope. This secret army of Jesuits aroused extraordinary alarm in the Elizabethan court and society. It was treasonable to shelter any of them.... Undeterred by such mortal consideration, Lady Cecily welcomed, under cover of night, a series of illicit tenants into Stonor. The most celebrated was the Oxford educated Jesuit, Edmund Campion.[10]

Campion began the printing of *Decem Rationes* from "Mount Pleasant", a secret hiding place above the main entrance to Stonor Lodge, which also contained a chapel and a back exit, for an emergency escape. In the spring of 1581, the surrounding countryside was filled with informers, spies, and secret agents. Campion and his associates could not be too careful. On June 27, four hundred copies of the *Decem Rationes* were secretly distributed in the benches of the University Church, Oxford, and attempts to capture Campion were greatly intensified.

---

[10] Leanda de Lisle and Peter Stanford, *The Catholics and Their Houses* (London: HarperCollins, 1995), 14.

In addition to the *Decem Rationes*, he had also written a challenging entreaty titled "Campion's Brag". This was circulated earlier than the author intended, and created an even greater stir throughout the countryside. It was an appeal to the intellectual classes of British society (the Privy Council, Parliament, and the universities), asking for a fair hearing of his case; if it had been circulated after his capture, it would have caused great sensation. As it was, the peroration Campion wrote for the "Brag" may have overstated the case, at least in the minds of his Jesuit superiors:

> And touching our Societie, let it be known to you that we have made league—all the Jesuits in the world, whose succession and multitude must overreach all the practices of England—cheerfully to carry the cross you shall lay upon us, and never to despair your recovery, while we have a man left to enjoy your Tyburn, or to be racked with your torments, or consumed with your prisons. The expense is reckoned, the enterprise is begun; it is of God, it cannot be withstood. So the faith was planted, so it must be restored.[11]

With the *Decem Rationes* and the "Brag" both public, it was becoming increasingly dangerous to remain at Stonor Park. Campion headed for Norfolk and on the way stopped for lodging at the home of one Mrs. Yates at Lyford, a safe haven, or so it seemed. On Sunday morning, July 16, 1581, Campion offered Mass for a congregation of about forty, among whom there was a traitor. The home was searched three times, and on the third day Campion was captured and taken with two other priests to the Tower of London. En

---

[11] Campion's "Brag", cited in Evelyn Waugh, *Edmund Campion* (Oxford: Oxford University Press, 1980), 117–18.

route, a conspicuous sign was pinned on him: "Campion, the seditious Jesuit".[12]

No amount of interrogation, even perhaps by the Queen herself, could persuade him to renounce his faith. Evelyn Waugh, one of Campion's biographers, describes the scene of his interrogation:

> They questioned him about his purpose in coming to England, about Persons, about his instructions from Rome. He answered easily and quietly; he had come for the salvation of souls. The harsh, preemptory tones of Elizabeth broke in; did he acknowledge her as his queen or not? Campion replied that he did indeed recognize her as his lawful queen and governess, and was bound to her in obedience in all temporal matters. She pressed him with the question of her deposition. He answered, with perfect candor, that it was a subject upon which theologians were still divided, and began to explain the distinction between the potestas ordinata and potestas inordinata of the Papacy, and quoted the text "render unto Caesar the things that are Caesar's".... But the politicians were not in the mood for a debate on Canon Law.... They were satisfied that he had no treasonable designs, and told him that they had no fault to find with him except that he was a Papist. "Which is my greatest glory," Campion replied.[13]

He was told in no uncertain terms that the past would be forgotten and there was no limit to the heights he could achieve if he would renounce Catholicism and enter the ministry. Waugh continues:

---

[12] Thurston and Attwater, *Butler's Lives of the Saints*, 4:468.
[13] Waugh, *Edmund Campion*, 157–58.

The offer was kind in its intention. They had no desire to kill the virtuous and gifted man who had once been their friend, a man, moreover, who could still be of good service to them. From earliest youth, among those nearest them, they had been used to the spectacle of men who would risk their lives for power, but to die deliberately, without hope of release, for an idea, was something beyond their comprehension.[14]

Campion was tortured beyond human endurance, yet he never lost his peace of soul or his ability to respond to every question, every objection, every insult. His had been a strong intellectual training, and his interrogators were no match for him:

A Jesuit, a Jebusite? Wherefore, I you pray?
Because he doth teach you the only right way?
He professeth the same by learning to prove
And shall we from learning to rack him remove?

His reasons were ready, his grounds were most sure
The enemy cannot his force long endure,
Campion, in camping on spiritual field
In God's cause his life is ready to yield.

Our preachers have preached in pastime and pleasure,
And now they be hated for passing all measure;
Their wives and their wealth have made them so mute,
They cannot nor dare not with Campion dispute.[15]

Finally, he was indicted on the charge that he, Cardinal Allen, and fellow Jesuits Persons and Morton formed a conspiracy to murder Queen Elizabeth and that he and Persons had been

---

[14] Ibid., 158.
[15] Cited in Waugh, *Edmund Campion*, 174.

chosen to precede the others to stir up a rebellion in support of their plan. Campion replied to these charges:

> 'I protest before God and His holy angels', before heaven and earth, before the world and this bar whereat I stand, which is but a small resemblance of the terrible judgement of the next life, that I am not guilty of any part of the treason contained in the indictment, or of any other treason whatever.[16]

Naturally, there was to be no fair trial. When the jury ultimately read the sentence of death, Campion responded in what has become a famous statement:

> In condemning us, you condemn all your own ancestors— all the ancient priests, bishops and kings—all that was once the glory of England, this island of saints, and the most devoted child of the See of Peter.[17]

Eleven days elapsed between his trial and his death. Though he remained in irons the entire time, his preparation for death was a very spiritually profitable one. On December 1, 1581, Edmund Campion, Ralph Sherwin, and Alexander Briant, all Jesuits, were brought together from the Newgate prison, where they had been incarcerated, to the hill of Tyburn, where they were executed with the usual barbarities. On the scaffold Campion refused to give an opinion of the Pope's Bull of Deposition against Queen Elizabeth and publicly prayed for her. While he was being executed, a young man named Walpole was sitting very close to the scene:

> He was a typical member of that easy-going majority, on whom the success of the Elizabethan Settlement depended,

[16] Ibid., 178–79.
[17] Ibid., 190.

who would have preferred to live under a Catholic regime, but accepted the change without very serious regret. . . . He secured a front place at Tyburn; so close that when Campion's entrails were torn out by the butcher and thrown into the cauldron of boiling water, a spot of blood splashed upon his coat. In that moment he was caught into a new life; he crossed the sea, became a priest, and, thirteen years later, after very terrible sufferings, died the same death as Campion's on the gallows at York.[18]

No surprise that a young man would be so moved by such a scene or by the man who was offering his life. This defender of the faith in Elizabethan England quickly became and still remains a tremendous source of pride for the Church, especially for the Society of Jesus, to which he gave his life: "For the Jesuits, Campion always heads the roll of honor; his genius and holiness were not to be challenged over four centuries."[19]

---

[18] Ibid., 198.

[19] Bernard Bassett, S.J., *The English Jesuits: From Campion to Martindale* (New York: Herder and Herder, 1968), 54.

IX

Philip Howard:
the Queen's Courtier

Lumen gentium, the Dogmatic Constitution on the Church of the Second Vatican Council, defines the laity as those faithful who by Baptism are

> made one body with Christ and ... established among the People of God. They are in their own way made sharers in the priestly, prophetic, and kingly functions of Christ. They carry out their own part in the mission of the whole Christian people with respect to the Church and the world.[1]

A sublime part they play is martyrdom. The *Catechism of the Catholic Church* defines martyrdom as "the supreme witness given to the truth of the faith". It goes on to state, "The martyr bears witness to Christ who died and rose, to whom he is united by charity.... He endures death through an act of fortitude." [2]

---

[1] *Lumen gentium*, no. 31, in Walter M. Abbot, S.J., ed., *The Documents of Vatican II* (New York: Herder and Herder/Association Press, 1966), 57.

[2] *Catechism of the Catholic Church*, 2d ed. (Vatican City: Libreria Editrice Vaticana, 1997), no. 2473.

Both definitions might be described as contemporary, coming as they do from the late twentieth century. They express timeless truths and are combined beautifully in the life of sixteenth-century dry martyr and devout Catholic layman Saint Philip Howard.

Philip was born into the finest British nobility. Christened for his godfather, King Philip II of Spain, he was the son of Thomas Howard, the fourth Duke of Norfolk, and Mary Fitzalan, daughter of the Earl of Arundel. His life centered around Arundel Castle, a fortress built in 1067 on the coast of Sussex. Philip Howard's descendants, the Dukes of Norfolk, have traditionally held the title of nobility associated with the old religion in England.

The saint was born on June 29, 1557, and baptized in the presence of Queen Mary Tudor by the last Catholic Archbishop of York, Nicholas Heath. Even then, Catholic power and influence was quickly slipping away in England; within weeks of Philip's birth, both Queen Mary and Reginald Pole, the last Catholic Archbishop of Canterbury, were dead. This did not augur well for Catholicism, though few realized it at the time. Nor was there much hope for Philip's own upbringing in the faith; his mother had never fully regained her health following childbirth and died when Philip was but two months old. She almost certainly would have raised her son in the Catholic faith. Following his first wife's death, Thomas Howard was to marry twice more: first, Margaret Audley, with whom he had two sons and a daughter, then Elizabeth Dacre, a widow with three daughters and a son. These marriages had brought the Duke wealth, property, and a large family, and he was determined his family would retain control of all their rightful holdings through the generations. His first two marriages had given him three sons and one daughter. His children would, therefore, marry the

Dacres; Philip, at the age of twelve, was betrothed to Anne Dacre. Though the union was very much arranged, it was a marriage "made in heaven", as far as Philip's ultimate sanctity was concerned.

While his children were still young, Thomas Howard purchased as a city dwelling the London Charterhouse, formerly occupied by the Carthusian monks who had been martyred during the reign of Henry VIII. The Duke would have had little sympathy with the Catholic heroes who once occupied the home, since he was much attracted to Protestantism and had little difficulty transferring his allegiance at the time of the Reformation. Initially, his son Philip seems to have taken after him, even to the point of religious indifference. Thomas Howard's third wife, Elizabeth, was, however, a very different case. When she was dying, her husband refused to allow a priest to visit her, though she longed for the consolation of the sacraments. Her mother, Lady Mounteagle, came to live with the Howards after Elizabeth's death and was equally determined that the children would be raised in the Catholic faith. In this she was aided greatly by Gregory Martin, a staunchly Catholic tutor whom Thomas Howard had engaged to help his children in their studies. Martin was a Fellow of Saint John's College at Oxford and would become the principal translator of the Douai Bible. Had the elder Howard known the Catholic influence Martin would be, he might have had second thoughts, since he continually professed a sincere and devout Protestantism.

Such loyalty was to avail him little in the end. Thomas Howard, Duke of Norfolk, was accused of involvement in a conspiracy to murder Queen Elizabeth I, possibly because of his intention to marry Mary, Queen of Scots, one of Queen Elizabeth's chief rivals. Howard steadfastly denied the allegations, but was imprisoned in the Tower of London and beheaded in 1572. Shortly before his death, he wrote to his son Philip, then a boy of fourteen, instructing him to

> [s]erve and fear God above all things. . . . Love and make much of your wife. . . . I wish you for the present to make your abode at Cambridge, which is the fittest place for you to promote your learning in. . . . Beware of the court. . . . When I am gone forget . . . and forgive . . . my false accusers . . . but have nothing to do with them if they live.[3]

Few sons ignored their father's admonitions more than Philip. The young man came under the strongly Protestant influence of Lord Burghley, one of the chief advisors to Queen Elizabeth. It was he who was responsible for Philip's admission to Cambridge (where he had a brilliant academic career), for introducing him at court, and for ridding him of the major Catholic influence in his life, his tutor Gregory Martin. Philip, for his part, became very taken with life at court. He was one of the Queen's favorites and often took part in skits, minstrels, and so forth, for the amusement of the woman who had signed his father's death warrant just a few years before.

Meanwhile, the other woman in his life, his wife, Anne Dacre, was being sorely neglected. His marriage, for a time, seemed to mean little to him:

> While the exact degree of his dissipation is difficult to know, there can be little doubt that at this time he was unfaithful to his wife. According to his first biographer, he patronized "corrupted, immodest young women with which the court in those times did too much abound".[4]

---

[3] Cited in Philip Caraman, S.J., *Saint Philip Howard* (London: Catholic Truth Society, 1985), 6.

[4] Ibid., 11.

Remorse eventually overcame him, especially in 1580, when his life took a far more serious turn. That year Philip became the thirteenth Earl of Arundel, following the death of his maternal grandfather, Henry Fitzalan. It meant he would take a greater interest in state affairs; it meant, too, that the years of court jesting were ended. His wife, Anne, was also changing, coming closer to her Catholic faith. At heart she never ceased to be a Catholic, though outwardly she conformed to the established church. She did attend Anglican worship, but always managed to avoid taking part in their "communion". What affected the change in her life was a book titled *The Dangers of Schism*. Upon completing it, she was convinced enough to seek out a priest and reconcile herself to the Catholic Church.

Philip Howard did not resist his wife's actions, despite the dire consequences that could result; he himself was undergoing a significant conversion. Shortly before the death of the Jesuit martyr Edmund Campion, Howard was present in the Tower and listened to Campion explain and defend his *Decem Rationes*, his ten reasons for being a Catholic, to a group of Protestant divines. Philip was deeply moved. Coincidentally, it was Howard's tutor, Gregory Martin, who years before had convinced Campion to confess publicly his Catholicism.

Two years of intense soul searching followed. Howard was at Arundel Castle when the stirrings of the Holy Spirit became evident in 1584: "Philip is supposed finally to have made up his mind on the religious question while pacing up and down his grandfather's long gallery in the east wing of the castle." [5] It was providential that the castle was strategically

---

[5] John Martin Robinson, *Arundel Castle* (Chichester: Phillimore, 1994), 16.

located on the coast, should escape become necessary. A Jesuit priest named William Weston (supposedly the only Jesuit freely moving about England) reconciled Howard to the Church, and it was a decision Philip would never regret. The conversions of Philip and Anne Howard did not go unnoticed at court. The Queen had long been envious of the time Philip spent with his wife, so as a gesture of conciliation, when their daughter was born they had her christened Elizabeth in the Anglican church, which was of no consequence to the Queen nor to the Howards.

Anne had never truly lost Catholic devotion and piety—Philip had. After his return to the faith he was a much-changed man, retaining a Catholic chaplain at the London Charterhouse, "by whom he could frequently receive the holy sacraments and daily have the comfort to be present at the Holy Sacrifice whereto with great humility and reverence he himself in person would many times serve".[6]

One of the means he chose to enhance his own Catholic spirituality was writing to Cardinal William Allen, founder of the English College at Douai, to inquire how he might help the Catholic cause. A reply came back urging Howard to flee England and its persecution and come to the Continent. Naturally, Howard, in good faith, assumed the reply came from the Cardinal. In fact, Philip's letter had been intercepted by a member of the Privy Council and the letter of response was a forgery. Father William Weston felt Howard's departure would weaken the position of the Catholics in England, since he served as a source of encouragement. Philip was of a mind to leave, however, and set his plans in motion.

---

[6] Cited in Caraman, *Saint Philip Howard*, 17.

Cardinal Allen was anything but imprudent; it would have been very risky to send a letter with just anyone. In fact, the letter was delivered by one Edward Crately, an apostate priest who had become friendly with the Howard family. He managed to convince Philip that he was making plans for his escape when, all the while, he was ensuring his arrest. The future saint would have much preferred to remain in England. His wife, Anne, was expecting their second child, and he knew what a toll the pain of separation would take on her. Still the greater Catholic interest seemed to justify Philip's going to the Continent.

When the evening of his departure arrived, he was detained several hours because of adverse winds— or so he was told. In fact, ships had been making safe channel crossings all evening. Finally, he departed from Lymington, a port in Hampshire, and no sooner had his ship left port than the captain hung a lamp over one side, a signal to those on a waiting vessel to come aboard and capture Howard. His possessions were confiscated, and he was taken under arrest to the Tower of London. The man who apprehended him was rewarded by being made a sheriff in Hampshire the following year.

Philip was brought before the Star Chamber and charged with three offenses: reconciling with Rome, attempting to flee the country, and correspondence with Cardinal Allen. Additionally, he was fined ten thousand pounds and confined to the Tower at the Queen's pleasure. The Queen believed the severity of his treatment would break Howard, and he would revert to being the loyal subject he had been. There were no courtesies extended him, and he was allowed only brief daily walks in what is called the Queen's Garden. For Philip, the result was quite opposite the Queen's expectations; he strengthened his resolution with daily set hours of prayer. Two hours each morning, an hour and a half in the afternoon, and a quarter of an hour before bed, given to the examination of his conscience.[7]

In all, Philip Howard would spend eleven years in the Tower of London, which is ironic since he had also spent eleven years of dissipation at court. His greatest sorrow was separation from his wife, Anne, who bore him a son shortly after his imprisonment. All attempts to see his wife and family were futile, though he was not completely without spiritual solace. A Jesuit priest, Robert Southwell, began a correspondence with him that has since been published as *An Epistle of Comfort*. The two men never met, but the thoughts Southwell expressed gave Philip great spiritual nourishment. The fact that the Jesuit was able to live in London in relative tranquility allowed him, among other things, to retain copies of his letters to Howard, which facilitated the eventual publication.

Early in 1587, Queen Elizabeth decided to take a more lenient approach with her prisoner. If harshness could not dissuade him, perhaps a gentler approach would. Not only could Philip visit with fellow prisoners in the Tower; he was even able to assist at Mass. Among the prisoners was at least one priest, and all necessary liturgical items were provided by the daughter of the Tower's lieutenant, a secret Catholic sympathizer. Several prisoners would gather on Sundays and major feasts to offer the Sacred Mysteries and most often Philip would serve.

In the 1580s, Britain was constantly on the alert for the possible arrival of an invasion by the Spanish Armada. Rumors prevailed that when the Armada landed, Britain would

[7] Ibid., 21.

retaliate with the slaughter of countless Catholics. When Philip and some of his fellow prisoners heard of this, their prayers were for the safety of their coreligionists. If the latter were captured, they prayed further that they be given sufficient spiritual preparation for death. This spiritual apostolate was picked up by Philip's enemies within the Tower and construed to mean he was praying and leading prayers for the success of the Spanish fleet. For this charge, he was finally brought to trial in 1589, in what could be described only as judicial travesty.

He had been in the Tower four years, and although thin and drawn, made an impressive appearance as he entered Westminster Hall for his trial. The inevitable verdict of guilty was rendered, and after sentence was pronounced, the Earl was asked if he had any requests; there were three: (1) that all his debts should be paid, (2) that he should be allowed to see his son, and (3) that his wife should be allowed to visit him. In hindsight, some historians have raised the question whether Elizabeth ever intended a death sentence be carried out. The furor of the crowd gathered for miles along the riverbank, venting their hostility against the government, would seem to bear out this view. Nonetheless, the prisoner's fate was kept a well-guarded secret.

> Not a bell that sounded that it might not be his knell; not a footstep was heard that it might not be the messenger of death. Each morning as he rose he knew not but that, before night, he might be a headless corpse; each night, as he laid his head upon his pillow, he was uncertain whether the morning light might not summon him to another world.[8]

---

[8] Cited in Caraman, *Saint Philip Howard*, 27.

Two years later, Catholics were just as fervent in their prayers for Philip's life. The fact that he knew many high-placed individuals in the Elizabethan court undoubtedly worked to his benefit. In addition, Robert Southwell kept up a correspondence until his own execution at Tyburn in February 1595. For his part, Philip was using his years in the Tower very profitably:

> When not praying or taking the air he devoted his time translating books of piety. *The Epistle of Jesus Christ to the Faithful Soul*, which he translated from the Latin, was the work of the Carthusian monk Johann Landsperger and went through many editions. It is known also that he wrote some devotional treatises, but only his *Fourfold Meditation on the Four Last Things* survives in some printed fragments. However, fourteen four-line stanzas of a poem entitled *Verses on Christ Crucified* are extant in their entirety.[9]

This said, it is also true that Philip was not a well man. He never lost hope that he might be permitted to see his family. At one point news reached him that Elizabeth was on the verge of granting his request, and she likely would have "if Philip would but once go to their church, not only would she grant his request, but he could be restored to his estates and honor with as much favor as she could show." [10] His biographer is quick to add: "Politely, but with great sorrow, Philip told the Lieutenant that he could not accept the Queen's offer on such conditions." [11]

[9] Ibid., 28.
[10] Ibid., 28–29.
[11] Ibid., 29.

Philip died in his cell on Sunday, October 19, 1595, at age thirty-eight. The night before he had said his Rosary and recited numerous Psalms from memory:

> Some have thought, and perhaps not improbably, that he had some foreknowledge of the day of his death because seven or eight days before, making some notes in his calendar, what prayers and devotions he intended to say on every day of the week following, when he came to the Sunday on which he died, he there made a pause, saying Hitherto and no farther, as the servants who then heard his words and saw him write have often testified.[12]

His body was first taken to the Tower chapel, only to have a Protestant clergyman eulogize rather curiously:

> We are not come to honour this man's religion. . . . We publicly profess and here openly protest otherwise to be saved, nor to honour his offence; the law has judged him, we leave him to the Lord, he hath gone to his place.[13]

Today one may venerate the relic of Philip Howard and pray at his tomb in Arundel Cathedral, very close to the castle where he lived. He was canonized by Pope Paul VI in 1970, along with Edmund Campion, Robert Southwell, and thirty-seven others. His wife, Anne, spent her remaining years on earth living a life of exemplary holiness and caring for the poor. Their son Thomas Howard lived a wasted life amid the glamor of the court and gave up his faith, only to return near the end of his life. By contrast, his son Viscount Stafford was martyred for the faith at the time of the Titus Oates plot

---

[12] Cited in Caraman, *Saint Philip Howard*, 29.
[13] Cited in Caraman, *Saint Philip Howard*, 29–30.

and became one of the last martyrs of the Reformation in England.

Philip Howard, though he never faced the scaffold, was a defender of the faith who died for the same very real principles. He proved true the words Robert Southwell once wrote to him in the Tower: "For your cause—by whatever name it may be disfigured—by whatever colour deformed in the eyes of men—is religion." [14]

[14] Cited in Caraman, *Saint Philip Howard*, 30.

X

The English Catholic Martyrs: Defenders in the Sixteenth Century

English martryology consists of many others who defended the faith by the witness of their lives. These men and women lived in various periods of British history, but were particularly numerous during the reign of Queen Elizabeth I (1558–1603). One such group, the Forty Martyrs of England and Wales, are especially remembered for the heroism of their lives and the unambiguous statement of faith seen in their deaths.[1]

They were canonized by His Holiness Pope Paul VI on October 25, 1970. In an address to a consistory of the College of Cardinals, the Holy Father gave his reasons for raising them to the altars of sainthood. These people had lived in times of great religious turmoil, but it was not the Church's

---

[1] The forty canonized saints are John Almond, Edmund Arrowsmith, Ambrose Barlow, John Boste, Alexander Briant, Edmund Campion, Margaret Clitherow, Philip Evans, Thomas Garnet, Edmund Gennings, Richard Gwyn, John Houghton, Philip Howard, John Jones, John Kemble, Luke Kirby, Robert Lawrence, David Lewis, Anne Line, John Lloyd, Cuthbert Mayne, Henry Morse, Nicholas Owen, John Pain, Polydore Plasden, John Plesington, Richard Reynolds, John Rigby, John Roberts, Alban Roe, Ralph Sherwin, Robert Southwell, John Southworth, John Stone, John Wall, Henry Walpole, Margaret Ward, Augustine Webster, Swithun Wells, and Eustace White.

intention to relive such controversy or reopen old wounds. Rather, the joy of canonization should provide opportunity for all Christians to reflect on the past and ask God's pardon for mutual misunderstanding and hostility:

> Whereas four hundred years ago this slaying of brother by brother could be conceived as an action pleasing to God, today, under the inspiration of God's grace, all men of good will are rightly horrified by such attitudes. They are fully determined that those who bear the name of Christ, the Prince of Peace, and the Shepherd of Souls, shall never again be permitted to be corrupted by such violence, or defiled by such bloodshed.[2]

At the same time the Holy Father reminded the entire Catholic world that these martyrs

> are a shining example of that genuine faith, which will have nothing to do with ambiguity or false compromise in whatever is held as sacred: a faith that is never afraid to declare its convictions. Such a faith is a necessary condition of all true and fruitful ecumenical dialogue.[3]

The Forty Martyrs were arrested, tried, convicted, sentenced, and put to death under the terms of three very broad, all-encompassing pieces of legislation, which allowed such leeway that there was not a situation that could not be held up as a violation of one of them. The Treason Act of 1352 had been passed during the reign of Edward III. By the time of the Reformation it still defined treason as plotting or at-

---

[2] Allocution of His Holiness Pope Paul VI to the College of Cardinals at the Consistory for the Canonization of the Forty English and Welsh Martyrs, May 18, 1961, cited in Clement Tigar, S.J., *Forty Martyrs of England and Wales* (London: Office of the Vice-Postulation, 1970), unnumbered.

[3] Ibid.

tempting to kill or dethrone the monarch or one of his descendants. An Act to Retain the Queen's Majesty's Subjects in Their Due Obedience was of more recent vintage, having passed in 1581; returning to the Church of Rome or being the cause of others' return constituted high treason. In addition, it defined the meaning of seditious words directed against the monarch. Finally, there was An Act against Jesuits, Seminary Priests and such other Disobedient Persons, which can trace its origins to June 24, 1559. Coming into effect in 1585, this law declared that any Catholic priest ordained abroad who later entered the realm was guilty of high treason; any who harbored or assisted such priests had committed a felony. Captured priests were to be hanged, drawn, and quartered, while lay people aiding or abetting them were to be hanged.

While most of the martyrs lived in Elizabethan times, some were earlier. John Houghton, Robert Lawrence, and Augustine Webster were the first martyrs of the English Reformation. They were the three Carthusians seen by Thomas More from his cell window in the Tower of London. More commented to his daughter Meg on how joyfully they were going to their deaths. The three Priors had asked Thomas Cromwell, the King's chief secretary, if some type of oath of allegiance could be given to them and their fellow Carthusians that would not violate their consciences. The request was quickly refused, and these men went to their deaths, always denying the charge of treason. How could they be guilty of treason, they queried, when it was impossible that a monarch, rather than a Pope, could be head of the Church?

Richard Reynolds had been described as "perhaps the most learned monk of his time, and certainly one of the holiest".[4]

---

[4] James Walsh, S.J., *Forty Martyrs of England and Wales* (London: Catholic Truth Society, 1997), 8.

He had been a Fellow of Corpus Christi College, Cambridge, and later joined the Bridgettine order. As one writer noted, "It was thought that if such a learned and saintly man were to accept the king as head of the church, this would put many consciences at rest." [5]

It did not happen. Reynolds was tendered the Oath of Supremacy (which recognized the King as head of the church), but refused to take it. He was tried with the three Carthusian Priors and martyred with them in 1535.

John Stone was an Augustinian priest stationed in the city of Canterbury and, like so many, ordered to take the Oath of Supremacy. He refused, and the details of that refusal were quickly related to the proper authorities. Stone had a lengthy imprisonment in the Tower of London, after which he was returned to Canterbury to stand trial. According to a friend, Father Stone had this experience while confined in Canterbury Castle:

> Having poured forth prayers in prison to God and fasted continuously for three days, he heard a voice though he saw no one, which addressed him by name and bade him to be of good heart and not to hesitate to suffer death with constancy for the belief which he had professed. From which afterwards he gained such eagerness and strength as never to allow himself by persuasion or terror to be drawn from his purpose. [6]

He never was, and his martyrdom in 1539 is proof positive.

The Jesuit Robert Southwell, friend of Philip Howard through correspondence, brings us further into the sixteenth century. Born in Norfolk in 1562, Southwell's back-

[5] Ibid.
[6] Nicholas Harpsfield, cited in Walsh, *Forty Martyrs*, 10.

ground on his father's side was not unlike that of Howard. The elder Southwell was a courtier of Elizabeth I and had no difficulty in conforming to the established church. Robert's mother was a devout Catholic who raised her son in the faith. He eventually went to the English College at Douai. Upon completion, he traveled to Belgium to seek admission to the Jesuits, but was refused. His desire to belong to the Society was so strong he went on foot to Rome, where he was admitted and finally ordained to the priesthood. When Southwell reentered England in 1586, he remained in London and labored there quite successfully for the next six years. In addition to his spiritual ministrations, he distinguished himself as a writer of prose and poetry. A young girl who had left the Catholic faith and had become a traitor knew his whereabouts and activities. Southwell was taken to the Tower of London to face intense torture; he was hanged, drawn, and quartered at Tyburn in 1595. His last thoughts were spoken in absolute sincerity:

> This is my death, my last farewell to this unfortunate life, and yet to me most happy and most fortunate. I pray it may be for the full satisfaction of my sins, for the good of my country, and for the satisfaction of many others. Which death, although it seems here disgraceful, yet I hope that in time to come it will be to my eternal glory.[7]

Another Jesuit from Norfolk, Henry Walpole, died the same year as Southwell and by the same means: he was hanged, drawn, and quartered. Walpole had been present at the execution of Edmund Campion, whose blood had spilled on Walpole's clothing. This event changed him completely. He became a Jesuit in Rome and was ordained to the priesthood

[7] Cited in Walsh, *Forty Martyrs*, 25.

in Paris in 1588. For a time he served as chaplain to the Spanish forces in the Netherlands and was briefly captured by the British but later set free. He longed for the English mission. In 1593, he reentered his native land, but he was captured within twenty-four hours. A brief imprisonment at York was followed by a far more severe incarceration in the Tower of London; he was tortured repeatedly in order that he give information about Catholics he knew in England and on the Continent, but he would not yield. A trial followed at York, and he was promised freedom if he would acknowledge the spiritual supremacy of the Queen. The freedom he chose was the glorious liberty of the sons of God.

Saints Cuthbert Mayne and Ralph Sherwin were contemporaries. Cuthbert is honored as the protomartyr of the English seminaries, while Ralph Sherwin is designated the protomartyr of the English College in Rome. Mayne was born in Devon, in the west county of England. He had studied at Oxford and taken orders in the established church. At the urging of Catholic friends (Edmund Campion among them), he returned to the Catholic faith and entered the English College at Douai, where he was ordained to the priesthood in 1575. After his return, he worked for one year in Cornwall. Finally, he was captured and arrested on the curious charge that he had brought a Papal Bull into England and was busy circulating it. He had been back in the land of his birth only two years at the time of his martyrdom.

Ralph Sherwin was native to Derbyshire. His student days at Rome's venerable English College on the Via Montserrat were preceded by studies at Exeter College, Oxford. He had conformed to Anglicanism, returned to the true faith, gone to the English College at Douai, and after ordination gone to the Eternal City for further studies. The Roman students were required to take an oath affirming their readiness to return to England as missionaries, and Sherwin's reply was said to have been "today, rather than tomorrow".[8] No sooner had the reality come than he was captured, put in chains in the Tower of London, and severely tortured. The depth of his spirituality allowed him to compare the noise of the chains to little bells whose melodious tunes delighted him. To his uncle he wrote, "Innocency is my only comfort against all the forged villainy which is fathered on my fellow priests and me."[9]

Ralph Sherwin was hanged, drawn, and quartered at Tyburn with Edmund Campion and Alexander Briant. Briant, for his part, was from Somerset and a product of the English Seminary at Douai. After his capture, for some reason, it was believed he would be a good source of information about other priests. As a result:

> For two days he was deprived of food and drink. His persecutors then thrust needles under his nails; ... he was cast for eight days into a pit twenty feet deep and without light. Then he was brought back to the torture chamber again and racked on two successive days until his body was disjointed. In all these sufferings he never revealed a single secret.... During his torture he promised God that he would seek admission to the Society of Jesus. He did so and was accepted before his death.[10]

Luke Kirby was an impetuous Yorkshireman. While traveling through Switzerland with Edmund Campion and Ralph Sherwin, he challenged a Calvinist to a debate, with the loser to suffer death (small wonder he would later be hunted).

[8] Tigar, *Forty Martyrs*, 20.
[9] Cited in Walsh, *Forty Martyrs*, 14.
[10] Ibid., 15.

Kirby was a product of Douai and later studied in Rome. He was hanged, drawn, and quartered at Tyburn in 1582.

Richard Gwyn was the first Welch martyr of Elizabeth's reign; a schoolmaster in Wales, he died for his refusal to acknowledge the Queen as head of the Church and for encouraging others to become Catholics.

Margaret Ward and Anne Line were among the women martyrs, though none of the women had as fascinating a story as Saint Margaret Clitherow. She was born and raised in the city of York, quite close to the famous York Minster Cathedral. Her father, Thomas Middleton, was a well-known, respected member of the City Corporation and Town Council, but he died rather young. Margaret's mother then married Henry May, a bit of an opportunist, who was eventually elected Lord Mayor. In 1571 Margaret married John Clitherow, a wealthy master butcher. They went to live in "The Shambles", a well-to-do street of traders, where their home may be seen to this day.

Margaret was raised a Protestant. It is not clear when she reconciled to the Catholic faith, but reconcile she did and at a great price. In the late sixteenth century the government imposed heavy fines and long prison sentences on those who did not attend Anglican worship. Margaret's husband, John, though not a Catholic, guarded his wife's religious faith closely. He once referred to her as "the best wife and the best Catholic in all the land", and his love for her kept him vigilant for her safety.

It was not uncommon in those days to have "pursuivants" come searching a suspect's home. Usually rough individuals in the government's employ, they would stop at nothing to earn extra money and often went looking for Mass items such as chalices, vestments, missals, and crucifixes. Margaret had all these and more in her home and also had enlisted the services of a priest (posing as a schoolteacher) to teach the faith to her children and those of her friends and neighbors. Catholic children were full well aware they could be persecuted for their faith, so they knew to be discreet. On one occasion, however, Margaret had invited the child of recently arrived Flemish immigrants who knew nothing of the situation in York. The pursuivants broke into her home, and the house was searched. The teacher managed to escape, but the little Flemish boy was captured and forced to tell all he knew and show the pursuivants where everything was hidden.

Margaret was imprisoned in York Castle along with her husband and her children. All but Margaret were eventually released. Her trial was in the Guildhall, where, as John Clitherow's wife, she had often attended banquets. It would not be a trial by jury, since she did not want her own children to be forced to testify against her. Instead, she was brought before a number of judges and four members of the Queen's Council for the North and charged with harboring traitor priests and attending Mass. Both were completely true, though Margaret refused to plead, claiming she had never committed any offense. She knew, of course, the guilty verdict awaiting her, and prominent a man as her husband was, he could do nothing for her. In fact, the council felt they had done him a great favor keeping him out of prison. Several Protestant ministers tried to persuade Margaret to change her mind, but to no avail.

Before her death, Margaret sent a pair of shoes to her daughter, Ann; she knew the girl would immediately grasp the meaning. She was telling her daughter to follow in her footsteps, and, in fact, she did. Ann spent two years in prison for her faith, but later went to Belgium, where she spent the remainder of her life in a religious community. As Margaret's own life draws to a close, a recent account takes up the story:

She prayed and trusted until it was time for her to be led out from the City, over the River Ouse, to the Toll Booth, a little hut, where she was put to death. She was to lie on the rough stone floor with a sharp boulder pressed into the small of her back. A heavy oak door would be laid over her and weights placed upon it until she was crushed to death.... After Margaret had prayed for the Queen and her executioners, and all those she loved, and protested that she had committed no crime except to obey her conscience in matters of religion, they started piling the weights upon her until her bones were broken, her internal organs crushed, and she could hardly breathe. Her last words, torn from her in gasps of agony, were "Jesus, Jesus, Jesus, have mercy on me." [11]

Margaret Clitherow died on the feast of the Annunciation, March 25, 1586. Her body was irreverently discarded, but faithful Catholics searched for weeks until they discovered it and gave it a reverent burial in a place that today has been lost to history. In the venerable English College in Rome there is a beautiful statue of Margaret Clitherow holding her Bible and carrying her housekeys. In her city of York, the famous Bar Convent is in possession of a relic that is believed to be her hand.

Margaret and her thirty-nine companions, who comprised the Forty Martyrs of England and Wales, are joined in English martyrology by the Lancaster Martyrs, some fifteen in number, so called because of the city in which they lost their lives.[12] They included both priests and laymen, all held

---

[11] Elizabeth Morris, *The Life and Death of Margaret Clitherow* (London: Catholic Truth Society, 1992), 8–9.

[12] Those who specifically died at Lancaster were Edmund Arrowsmith, Laurence Bailey, Edward Bamber, Ambrose Barlow, James Bell, John Finch, Richard Herst, Thurston Hunt, Robert Middleton, Robert Nutter, John Thules, Edward Thwing, Thomas Whitaker, John Woodcock, and Roger Wrenno.

prisoner in Lancaster Castle, all executed at a place called Gallows Hill.

James Bell and John Finch were both executed in 1584. Bell had been educated at Oxford and was ordained a priest in England. During the reign of Queen Mary Tudor, he had the distinction of being the only "Marian priest" among the group; the others were all "seminary priests", that is, they were ordained in English seminaries on the Continent. One author notes that it "was custom to imprison rather than to execute Marian priests; few of them died violently, and James Bell was thus an exception".[13]

Bell had been an Anglican minister for twenty years, when a devout Catholic lady of Lancashire persuaded him to return. He did, but was soon captured and imprisoned. John Finch, his fellow prisoner in the dock, was the first layman to die in Lancaster who

> was reconciled to the Catholic church in his twenties while managing his wife's farm in Lancashire, and thereupon set himself the onerous but valuable task of conducting from one Catholic house to another, priests endeavoring to carry on their ministry, under the difficult conditions of the time.[14]

After the inevitable condemnation of both men came, the two spent their final hours spiritually preparing for their deaths; the layman made his confession to the priest. "When the dawn came they blessed the day; Bell called it the fairest he had ever seen in his life." [15]

---

[13] Canon J. E. Bamber, *The Lancaster Martyrs* (London: Catholic Truth Society, n.d.), 3.

[14] Ibid., 4.

[15] Ibid., 5.

It was not until 1600 that two more Lancaster martyrs, Robert Nutter and Edward Thwing, were hanged, drawn, and quartered for their priesthood. Eight months later, Thurston Hunt and Robert Middleton, fellow Yorkshiremen and both priests, lost their lives. On the Privy Council's orders, these men were transported to London and returned to Lancaster, all the while treated with much severity. In the end,

> Mr. Hunt was first executed and, having the corde about his neck, he gave his blessing to all Catholicks there present, which were a great number. Both were executed in their cassocks. Mr. Hunt hanged till he was dead. Mr. Middleton seemed to have flown up the gallows, he went so nimbly up and was cut downe alive by error, as some think. For as soon as the rope was cutt and he began to stirre in the butcher's hands, the sheriff bid streightwaies cutt off his head, and soe it was; and thus he, beinge last hanged, was first quartered. Everyone lamented their death, for all the world perceived their innocency; and not only Catholicks but schismaticks of all sortes strived to have something of theirs for relicks.[16]

By 1628, the Lancaster Martyrs could count Edmund Arrowsmith among their number. A Lancashireman who had studied at Douai, he worked as a secular priest in his native area of England for over a decade. Rather outspoken, an early biographer said that he "often wished him merrily to carry salt in his pocket to season his actions, lest too much zeal without discretion might bring him too soon into danger".[17]

It surely did. He was imprisoned but later released. He entered the Society of Jesus in 1624 and returned to Lancashire until he was finally recaptured. Before his death, he

---

[16] Father Christopher Grene, S.J. (1629–1697), cited in Walsh, *Forty Martyrs*, 8–9.

[17] Cited in Walsh, *Forty Martyrs*, 46.

received absolution from his fellow prisoner, Saint John South-worth, whose remains may be venerated to this day at West-minster Cathedral, London. Southworth would outlive Arrowsmith many years, only to die a similar martyr's death at Tyburn.

Such is a sampling of the great people who gave their lives at Lancaster, and those of Elizabethan times and earlier whose defense of the faith was second to none. The blood of the early Christian martyrs is described as the seed of the church. The blood of the English martyrs may well be a significant seed of faith, which our contemporary culture so desperately needs.

XI

Hilaire Belloc: A Modern Defender

At the time of Hilaire Belloc's death in 1953, one admirer felt he had done more than any of his contemporaries to establish a Catholic presence in the world. His close friend G. K. Chesterton viewed him as a man interested only in good things, to the point of giving his all to fight for them. What he wished most to be remembered for, Belloc had written on his epitaph:

> I challenged and I kept the Faith,
> The bleeding path alone I trod;
> It darkens. Stand about my wraith,
> And harbour me—almighty God.[1]

Hilaire Belloc was a novelist, essayist, poet, politician, journalist, and historian. More than these, he was a Catholic apologist, a modern defender of the faith. He was born just a short distance from Paris in the village of La Celle St. Cloud, on July 27, 1870. His mother, Elizabeth Parkes, a great-granddaughter of the English scientist Joseph Priestley, was raised a Unitarian in Birmingham. She made a visit to Ire-

[1] Kevin L. Morris, *Hilaire Belloc:A Catholic Prophet* (London: Catholic Truth Society, 1995), 19.

land in 1864 and was so impressed with the faith of the people she became a Catholic. Three years later she married French barrister Louis Belloc; during their brief married life they alternated their time between La Celle St. Cloud and London. Louis Belloc had been in poor health for some years and died quite suddenly in 1872, which would be the beginning of a dire financial situation for his wife and family. Within six years, Mrs. Belloc left France with her children and moved to England, to Slindon in Sussex.

> This was Belloc's first acquaintance with the county which was later to play so important a part in his life and his writings. For two years he passed the greater part of his time there with his mother in undisturbed enjoyment of the beauty of the surroundings.[2]

At age ten Belloc was sent as a boarder to Birmingham's Oratory School, which had been founded by Cardinal Newman. He would remain there for seven years, excelling in his school work, taking part in student-led Latin plays, and filling his mind with all sorts of ideas, which, even at this early age, he was determined to express in writing. His mother was of a different mind; to her, journalism seemed an unstable financial life. Instead, she preferred to have her son work the soil. She apprenticed him to a gardener working on the large estate surrounding Arundel Castle, ancestral home of the Duke of Norfolk. The success of this was unlikely from the start; Belloc always maintained an interest in agriculture, but his mind was too full of literature and politics to be satisfied with a bucolic existence.

---

[2] Eleanor and Reginald Jebb, *Testimony to Hilaire Belloc* (London: Methuen and Company, 1956), 6.

In 1889 Belloc met Elodie Hogan, the woman he would marry seven years later. The Hogans had immigrated to California during the famine in Ireland nearly one half century earlier. Now, Elodie and her sister were on holiday in England and had the opportunity to meet Mrs. Belloc. Seven years had elapsed before marriage because of Elodie's vacillation. She had felt the call to a religious vocation and had spent some time in a Baltimore convent. In the end, she chose married life.

During these years of waiting, Belloc did a brief tour in the military and then began studies at Balliol College, Oxford, where he had won a scholarship and had an impressive academic career. He became skilled as a speaker and as a historian. His speaking ability allowed him to become president of the Oxford Union; his historical acumen won for him the Brakenbury scholarship in history, and his complete academic record accounted for the "brilliant first"[3] he received upon completing his course work. He was expecting a college Fellowship, allowing him the life of a don. Competition was stiff, and when he did not get it, there was a certain disappointment. In retrospect, it worked out well. A don's life was a somewhat limited one, and the variety of Belloc's interests, not to mention his tremendous mental energy, may well have been stifled.

At its beginnings, his writing career was partially pragmatic—he had to make a living. He began with a book of verse, but was quickly dissatisfied with it and took it out of circulation. There followed books on the French Revolution, one on Paris, which displayed a fine knowledge of

[3] Ibid., 8.

the city's background, and the long-remembered *Path to Rome*, depicting his meandering on foot to the Eternal City.

Belloc had been living in the Chelsea section of London, but moved to Sussex in search of a permanent home for himself and his family. He found one at King's Land, near West Grinstead. King's Land was his home until his death; it is very close to the Shrine Church of Our Lady of Consolation, and in the graveyard today can be seen the graves of Hilaire and Elodie Belloc. In the centuries-old rectory can be found a hiding place for persecuted priests during the Reformation.

As the nineteenth century gave way to the twentieth, Belloc would do a great deal of writing at King's Land. In addition, he served in Parliament as a member of the Liberal Party, but his chagrin over many of the happenings in the body caused him to resign. Later he expressed many of his disagreements concerning politics in a publication called *The Eyewitness*. He became subdued, however, following the death of his wife, Elodie, in 1914. Belloc never got over her death; he dressed in black the remainder of his life. He produced scant literary output for several years until the time he was turned down by the army for military service during the First World War and was later persuaded by a friend to begin writing for a war publication called *Land and Water*. In its pages he wrote numerous articles on the war's progress and made several visits to the front lines to lend even greater veracity to what he wrote. The review became enormously popular, and Belloc could not keep up with the invitations he received to lecture on the strategy and tactics of the war throughout England.

The remaining decades of his life were much the same as his earlier years: history and politics presented in lecturing and writing. To these he added apologetics, and in his approach to each, Belloc's strong faith is dominant:

He saw the world, not as a conglomeration of races and disparate individuals, but as a place in which men and women fall into two groups: on the one hand those who had received the gift of faith and knowledge of the truth; on the other, those who pursue a medley of will-o'-the-wisps, each deviating in one way or another from the truth, and hence deceptive and harmful. That conviction colored all his writing.[4]

Belloc felt that traditional British historical writing was blatantly anti-Catholic. Human progress was viewed as a movement away from any form of Catholic dominance, in particular, any evolution from the Middle Ages, in which the Church had exercised such a powerful role. In response to such historiography, Belloc wanted to produce an authentically Catholic history, one that viewed the Church as the only real source of truth, goodness, and genuine progress the world had ever known. In this, he has been described as more a publicist than a historian:

In his enthusiasm he was often over emphatic, simplistic, judgmental and erroneous.... His histories were true in their soul, if not always in their substance. He was certainly interested in historical facts, and frequently argued in pursuit of them; but he was primarily interested in facts as building blocks for his mystical temple; so that though his facts were sometimes wrong, they were never lies. His histories should be read, then, not so much for their facts—though there are plenty of those—but for his vision of what the facts should be.[5]

[4] Ibid., 64.
[5] Morris, *Hilaire Belloc*, 7.

It took Belloc six years (1925–1931) to complete his *History of England*. At the same time he was writing *How the Reformation Happened* (1928) and *Wolsey* (1930). From the time of the conversion of the Roman Empire to Christianity until the twentieth century, he believed the Reformation to be the most significant event, if not the most catastrophic. It resulted

> in the destruction of Christendom's unity, the elimination of medieval liberties and democratic structures, the dispossession of the poor by the rich, the development of an astonishing individualism and the creation of a new oligarchy which evolved into the industrial, capitalist class.[6]

Belloc was intent on debunking what he considered a myth: that the Reformation was a popular, liberating movement. In England it had been the rich and powerful classes in society rebelling against the Church, and the success of that rebellion strongly affected the continent of Europe. His 1920 book *Europe and the Faith* was characteristic of this. The Catholic Church had been an intrinsic part of European civilization from the beginning, molding its character and shaping its soul, and France had become the "eldest daughter of the Church". Those who tried to "reform" what the Church had been for centuries were the real strangers and intruders. Belloc concluded this work with a statement for which he will long be remembered: "The Faith is Europe. And Europe is the Faith."[7]

In its relations with Catholic Europe, Britain had become almost isolationistic. Belloc was trying to clear the path for

[6] Ibid., 8.
[7] Hilaire Belloc, *Europe and the Faith* (London: Constable and Company, 1924), 331.

his countrymen to travel to their true home. He had made the point that the Church had saved Roman society, and implicit in that point was another: the Church could do the same for England in the twentieth century. He had written *Europe and the Faith* and many of his historical works specifically for English Catholics; those Irish who had lived in Great Britain for generations and made up a large concentration of the Catholic population; converts who had come over primarily from the Church of England; and recusants, who belonged to traditional English Catholic families loyal to Rome since the Reformation. One biographer noted that in this particular area "no one did more [than Belloc] to give the English Catholics confidence in themselves, and to make them feel part of a European tradition." [8]

As a liberal Member of Parliament for five years (1906–1911), Belloc had supported many Liberal Party initiatives and candidates. He used this opportunity to speak up occasionally on Catholic issues, such as education and the question of Ireland. He always felt the church should remain neutral regarding specific forms of government, though in England the established church was strongly intertwined with government, the richest and most powerful individuals were almost exclusively Church of England members, and their political and economic priorities seemed almost sacrosanct. Surely, they were not open to criticism from Catholicism, the most foreign of bodies, even if what they advocated was at variance with Catholic social or moral principles.

Shortly after leaving Parliament, Belloc became a close friend of the English Dominican Father Vincent McNabb. Each man seemed to fuel the other's energy to express his

[8] Robert Speaight, *The Life of Hilaire Belloc* (London: Hollis and Carter, 1957), 384.

feelings concerning the excesses of British capitalism and the rights of the poor to property. This had often been a theme in Belloc's writings, and it reached its most fervent expression in 1912 with the publication of *The Servile State*. He strongly asserted that the Liberal's concept of the welfare state was a plan to make the poor complacently passive and victims of what he termed "wage slavery". The popularity of this notion in the British mind could be attributed only to the decline of Catholicism. Liberals were to blame the most, but Conservatives and Socialists fared little better in Belloc's indictment.

A far more Christian concept, one that Belloc shared with his friend G. K. Chesterton, was the idea of Distributism, in which a co-operative society distributes finances and the means of production to the poor to provide them their rightful dignity:

> The most pressing moral problem was the "vile cancer of capitalism," with its ambiance of ephemeral and empoisoned chaos; and it was a moral issue because the control of wealth was the control of life.[9]

Belloc was one of many English Catholics strongly influenced by Pope Leo XIII's 1891 encyclical on the rights of labor, *Rerum novarum*. Their guiding principles seemed to view the poor as very close to God and the rich as religiously indifferent. Having a great fortune tended by its very nature to corrupt,

> "it is always to the advantage of the wealthy to deny general conceptions of right and wrong:" and people were even deluded into equating wealth with righteousness, when, in fact,

[9] Morris, *Hilaire Belloc*, 11.

the pursuit of wealth tended to usurp the pursuit of God. He condemned as "monstrous" the philosophy which suggested that the indefinite extension of private greed would work out to the advantage of all.[10]

With one stroke of the pen, Belloc could be sharply critical of a large segment of the population, but many of his critics would undoubtedly charge that by the economic standards of his day he was a man of comfortable means. There was a great distance between that, however, and the forgetfulness of God. Belloc would not have criticized the individual initiative of hard work, which provided financial success; he would strongly criticize the greed, which ignored others and forgot God.

In both historical and economic views, then, his faith was all pervasive. In his defense of that same faith he was a man who "wanted to give his fellow Catholics the courage to speak up, and to make the world respect and listen to the Church".[11]

He once said that "Catholicism is never more alive than when it is in arms",[12] and his heroes tended to be those who defended the faith with great intellectual, moral, and political fervor. Many of his coreligionists who read him were far less enthusiastic. They felt a more prudent course was peaceful coexistence, in return for which they would be tolerated and allowed to live securely in Britain. Hilaire, on the other hand, never lost the vitality and vibrancy of his faith once he had achieved it. As a young man it had not been nearly so strong, only with years did it develop. By 1922, when his

[10] Ibid.
[11] Ibid., 18.
[12] Cited in Morris, *Hilaire Belloc*, 16.

friend G. K. Chesterton converted to Catholicism, he could write:

> I am by all my nature of mind, skeptical.... But I accept these phrases as true and act upon them as well as a struggling man can. And as to the doubt of the soul, I discover it to be false: a mood: not a conclusion. My conclusion—and that of all men who have ever once *seen* it—is the Faith. Corporate, organized, a personality, teaching. A thing, not a theory. It.[13]

Belloc believed the Church, the Mystical Body of Christ, was a living reality in the contemporary world. It was the one bridge between time and eternity, something completely extraworldly and autonomous. Hence, it could never be tied to anything in the temporal order, as so many Christian denominations were. The Church could speak with a real authority, provide humanity a map of life that was clear and unambiguous, and give to all people the means necessary to work out their eternal salvation. The Church was reality; everything outside of it, a distortion. He described Catholic practice as "right [ordered], sane and normal", and all deviation from it stemmed from the excesses of heresy. His conclusion is not surprising:

> The moral is, it is indeed,
> you cannot monkey with the Creed.[14]

This characteristic of wholeness and very strict doctrinal orthodoxy did not preclude change. Where that change was

---

[13] Hilaire Belloc to G. K. Chesterton, August 1922, cited in Speaight, *Life of Hilaire Belloc*, 374.

[14] Cited in Frank J. Sheed, *The Church and I* (Garden City, N.Y.: Doubleday and Company, 1974), 100.

constructive, "for my part, I rejoice at new things. They are to me the proof of life. . . . These . . . are part of a living thing in which I am: not a document nor a mere record." [15]

It is not surprising that atheists and agnostics were not to be found among his closest friends. Nonetheless, he never shied away from a spirited debate with anyone, including such personalities as George Bernard Shaw and H. G. Wells. The latter was well known for his anti-Catholicism, yet Belloc believed passionately in the truth of the Church and in spreading that truth in a land that knew so little about it. His friend J. B. Morton once remarked that Belloc was never one to "wear his religion on his sleeve", which makes it all the more significant that he advanced the Catholic position in England to the degree he did.

Belloc had a chapel in his home at King's Land, with the Blessed Sacrament reserved. It gave him great delight whenever a priest was available to offer the Holy Sacrifice of the Mass, though as a participant he was not always the most recollected. Frank Sheed, his friend and the publisher of many of his books, remembered that "he moved about in his chair, muttered, could not take the Mass quietly. There were moods indeed in which he could not take anything quietly." [16] This was evident on many occasions in his life, but one is especially noteworthy. Mr. Sheed continues:

When a side chapel was being opened to Chesterton's memory in the church at Beaconsfield, there was a great crowd down from London. One could hardly breathe for the press of people standing. Suddenly there was a commotion in the back of the church. It was Belloc demanding to go to con-

[15] Cited in Morris, *Hilaire Belloc*, 15.
[16] Sheed, *The Church and I*, 111.

fession. He thrust his way through. As he passed me, I heard him say, "It's not essential, but it's urgent." He went into the sacristy, told the altar boys to clear out, and made his confession there and then to the priest already vested for the altar.[17]

He was not a man given to a plethora of pietistic practices or devotional exercises, except Benediction of the Blessed Sacrament. Rather, as Sheed has remarked, it was the body of the Church that really held Belloc. He considered any dissension within that body useless, counterproductive, and at variance with the mind of Christ.

He served that body faithfully and well. In 1934, Pope Pius XI noted the value of his work by making him a Knight Commander of Saint Gregory. Illness diminished his capacities in his latter years, though he never completely lost his earlier high spirits. Upon his death in 1953, Monsignor Ronald Knox judged that he had truly been "a prophet by destiny and by temperament [with] a pitiless insight into the structures of those things we take for granted".[18]

Frank Sheed was perhaps even more to the point:

A wonderful personality ... so rich and various that his opponents could not cope with him. ... All this went into his battle for the faith. The devotion, the learning, the gaiety, the grandeur, the courage. ... The total effect was magnificent, and we are all so deep in his debt that our best thanks are feeble in comparison.[19]

[17] Ibid.
[18] Cited in Morris, *Hilaire Belloc*, 5.
[19] Ibid.

XII

Catholic Truth Society and Catholic Evidence Guild: Defense of the Faith in Print and Word

The Catholic Truth Society and the Catholic Evidence Guild, two apologetic groups who can trace their origins to England, to the late nineteenth and early twentieth centuries, have defended the faith extremely well through the printed and spoken word. The first to be established was the Catholic Truth Society, which had two periods of existence.

The Society's origins go back to the time when long before entering the episcopacy, then Father Herbert Vaughan founded and served as Rector of Saint Joseph's Missionary Seminary at Mill Hill, London. It was during his service at the seminary that Vaughan had seen the tremendous need for the spread of the gospel, which prompted him to begin an organization to disseminate pamphlets explaining the Catholic faith to average readers. Others before Vaughan had similar visions; smaller tract societies had come and gone, but Father Vaughan's was to succeed. He believed his endeavor would serve to instruct Catholics in their own faith and break down a great deal of prejudice in the non-Catholic mind. In

1868 Father Vaughan purchased a publication called *The Tablet* and began to advance the need for the Catholic Truth Society. Protestant organizations were distributing fifty to sixty million pamphlets per year in the British Isles; now the fullness of faith would find similar expression. Vaughan was clear on the workings of the Society:

> On Sundays, many of these tracts will be distributed ... in the streets, in parks and other places of public resort ... at church doors, in the cottages of our country population, in the courts of our great towns where our poor are crowded; while on other days a certain number of respectable men and women of the poorer classes may be employed as hawkers for the purpose of sale and distribution.[1]

London, of course, would be Society headquarters. The term "auxiliary houses" was given to foundations in some of Britain's principal cities: Liverpool, Birmingham, Manchester, Preston, and Leeds. Hopeful as these plans were, they were largely abandoned in 1872 when Vaughan was appointed Bishop of Salford; an understandable preoccupation with his episcopal duties precluded his direct involvement. It would be twelve years until the Society was reorganized, when in October 1884, Bishop Vaughan wrote to Lady Herbert of Lea and asked: "Would you mind a committee of the Catholic Truth Society meeting at your home November 5th at 3 pm and taking part yourself? We are reviving it, and this time I think it will succeed." [2] It was reorganized under the guidance of James Britten, a devout Catholic layman.

---

[1] Christopher Ralls, *The Catholic Truth Society: A New History* (London: Catholic Truth Society, 1993), 2.

[2] Bishop Herbert Vaughan to Lady Herbert of Lea, October 24, 1884, cited in Msgr. George Stack, ed., *Westminster Cathedral: 1895–1995* (London: Westminster Cathedral, 1995), unnumbered.

Britten was in an advantageous position; at age thirty-eight, this former medical student was unmarried and full of the zeal that so often identifies new converts. He had come from a high Anglican background, but found lacking in the Anglican church any real claim to authority on the part of its clergy and any clearly defined teaching. Britten was the leading figure to emerge at the 1884 meeting called by Bishop Vaughan. On that fall afternoon, Britten and Monsignor William Cologan became joint secretaries, the name Catholic Truth Society was formally adopted, and the particulars of organization were agreed upon. Sometime later, the Society more formally defined its aims:

1. To disseminate among Catholics small and cheap devotional works.
2. To assist the uneducated poor to a better knowledge of their religion.
3. To spread among Protestants information about Catholic Truth.
4. To promote the circulation of good, cheap, and popular Catholic works.[3]

Much success would lie in the years ahead. Although membership never grew exceedingly large, the cheap price of one penny per pamphlet and the invention of the church-door rack, where such pamphlets could be placed, ensured the sale and distribution of thousands of pieces of Catholic literature throughout the British Isles. A Manchester priest, Father Charles Rothwell, had the idea of placing such door cases in church vestibules, an idea that has remained popular since its inception in 1887.

[3] Ibid., 7.

The Catholic Truth Society benefited in another area. There were few publishing companies in England, if any at all, that were interested in cornering the market for penny pamphlets on the Catholic faith, leaving the field clear. In the first quarter-century of the Society's existence, six million pamphlets were sold, of which *The Simple Prayer Book* sold two million. Other highly successful publications were a pamphlet refuting the *Awful Disclosures of Maria Monk*, a piece of sensational fiction supposedly written by an ex-nun, supposedly telling all the unspeakable scandals that occurred in Hotel Dieu Nunnery in Montreal. Also, Cardinal John Henry Newman's *Present Position of Catholics in England* was reprinted often, due to great demand.

With sales soaring, the Society's directors turned their attention to membership. They felt the creation of an Organizing Secretary might boost numbers. The man chosen was George Elliot Anstruther. "[E]loquent, tireless, indomitable", as one member described him, Anstruther would serve the Society with distinction until 1920. Anstruther had anything but a nine to five, Monday through Friday job:

> Many a time, on a wet Saturday night, he trampled around the streets of some northern industrial town, looking for the school room or temperance hall in which he could deliver an address. He would stay the night at the local presbytery, and return to London by a slow train on the Sunday evening.[4]

Men like Britten and Anstruther were conspicuous for their faith and activity; though membership was never what they hoped, the number of reported conversions among people reading Catholic Truth Society pamphlets was especially

---

[4] Ibid., 11.

rewarding. These dominant personalities were joined by another in 1912. William Reed-Lewis had moved to London from the United States and had begun a large, centrally located Catholic library, in which all his family worked. He naturally came to the attention of Britten, who invited him to join the Society. There would be considerable friction between the two men until Britten's death in 1924. Reed-Lewis had grandiose plans to extend the Society's headquarters to a prominent location on Victoria Street, London. The new offices would include a large reading room and an information bureau. Britten viewed the entire plan as too expensive and contrary to the Society's original purpose. Further complicating matters, Reed-Lewis began a new publication called *Catholic Truth*, which Britten also felt unnecessary. Also, Reed-Lewis had been editing *Catholic Book Notes* for several years. Although Reed-Lewis argued that the publication aimed at two different reading audiences, Britten was not to be convinced. In the end, the two publications merged, hoping to reach both groups, and the Society went on.

In 1929, to commemorate the centenary of Catholic Emancipation, the Society expanded its History and Biography sections. By mid-century, its director was Thomas Hardwick Rittner. A graduate of Ampleforth Abbey, Oxford, and the University of Bonn, he would receive the Pro Ecclesia et Pontifice Cross for his more than quarter-century dedication to the faith. In 1950, another centenary was observed: the restoration of the Catholic hierarchy in Great Britain. Rittner directed a magnificent exhibition called "Catholic England". These years would also mark the Society's entrance into the marketing of Scripture. In 1956 they received a generous, anonymous gift, allowing them to publish a popular edition of the Douai Bible, comparable in price and quality with similar editions by other Bible societies. Then in 1964, their prestige rose even higher when Pope Paul VI granted them the title "Publishers to the Holy See". It enhanced their position to obtain sole right to publish the Revised Standard Version of the Bible in paperback. By the mid-1970s they were circulating three million publications a year and three thousand churches throughout the British Isles had Catholic Truth Society bookracks in their vestibules.

Personalities came and went and locations changed, but the Catholic Truth Society objectives remained the same. The Cardinal Archbishops of Westminster traditionally served as the Society's president, and when Herbert Vaughan succeeded to the see, they had a very interested successor. In varying degrees that was true of each of his successors, including George Basil Hume, O.S.B. Following the election of Pope John Paul II, Cardinal Hume had the foresight to recommend the Society begin publishing *The Pope Speaks*. The Cardinal, knowing the brilliant intellect of the new Polish Pope, sensed a prolific output, which proved to be correct. This publication was joined by yet another, called *The Catholic*. These, along with the familiar pamphlets on the faith, have ensured the Society's success into the twenty-first century. More importantly, the faith continues to be presented to millions with the same eagerness and loyalty to the Holy See.

What the Catholic Truth Society did for the defense of the faith in print, the Catholic Evidence Guild accomplished from the lecture platform. It, too, began in London under the direction of a devout Catholic New Zealander, Vernon Redwood. Established specifically for the apostolate of street teaching, it had the permission and encouragement of Francis Cardinal Bourne of Westminster. Speakers' Corner at Marble Arch, Hyde Park, a "well-known spot for the ventilation of ideas",[5] is where the pioneer members did their initial evangelizing. A row of platforms would always be found at Speakers' Corner, and every political, social, and religious opinion could eventually get a hearing. The Guild was identified by a sign and had a standing crucifix next to the speaker. Its object and purposes were clearly underscored by at least two of its members:

> The object . . . is to teach anyone who wants to listen about the Catholic faith. We gather our audience in Hyde Park in London, in the Bull ring in Birmingham, at the Pier Head in Liverpool, in the Domain in Sydney, on Wall Street or Times Square in New York, at street corners everywhere. And not with speakers only, with listeners too, we get down to the bedrock of humanity and discover in day-to-day experience how much more important it is to belong to the human race than to any special section. Our chief novelty as street preachers was that we aimed at the mind, not the emotions.[6]

Continuing in this vein, another Guild member declared:

> We were there to introduce people to Christ's Church. We were not prettying the Church for its photograph. Still less were we like lawyers with a shady client, trying to keep his worst crimes from the jury's knowledge. We had to show them the Church Christ founded exactly as it was and is. If they were scandalized by what they saw, they must take it up with Christ who founded it, or with the Holy Spirit who vivifies it.[7]

---

[5] Maisie Ward, *Unfinished Business* (London: Sheed and Ward, 1964), 18.
[6] Ibid., 82.
[7] Frank Sheed, *The Church and I* (Garden City, N.Y.: Doubleday and Company, 1974), 63.

The first definition was given by Maisie Ward, one of the Guild's founders; the second by her husband, Frank Sheed, whom she met through their mutual Guild work. Maisie Ward was the granddaughter of William George Ward, a keen intellect, an Oxford Movement convert, and editor of the *Dublin Review.* Her father, Wilfred Ward, was a distinguished writer and biographer of Cardinal Newman. Her husband, Frank Sheed, was an Australian of Irish descent who earned his law degree at the University of Sydney. He became one of the Guild's most knowledgeable and sought-after speakers; in later years as a writer he would become famous for his ability to present theology, history, and philosophy in a clear, understandable style. He wrote some twenty books, among them the best-selling *Theology and Sanity* (1946), a translation of the *Confessions of Saint Augustine* (1943), *Theology for Beginners* (1957), and *To Know Christ Jesus* (1962). His wife, Maisie Ward, authored a series of biographies, the best known of which were *Gilbert Keith Chesterton* (1943), *Return to Chesterton* (1952), and *Young Mr. Newman* (1948). The couple had married in 1926, the same year they began the publishing house of Sheed and Ward, on Maiden Lane in London. They expanded it to New York City in 1933 and built it into one of the largest Catholic publishing houses in the world. Prior to their deaths (hers in 1975, his in 1981), they each wrote their memoirs, and from these sources we catch a glimpse of the Catholic Evidence Guild they served so faithfully.

The Guild was intended to be diocesan in character, the first being established in Westminster. Maisie Ward recalled the early years under Cardinal Bourne:

A certain reserve and coldness of manner masked the immense courage and generosity of which the Cardinal was capable. There was very much opposition to the idea of the Guild among the old fashioned clergy and laity—it was a danger to the Church to have laymen speaking publicly, a degradation to the Church to resort to these Salvation Army methods. Quietly, with an occasional pull that reminded us he held the reins, the Cardinal supported us. When we published the first edition of our *Training Outlines*, he wrote the introduction—suggesting that priests might find the book useful in preparing their sermons. It is hard today to realize how revolutionary such a remark appeared.[8]

Lectures on Catholic apologetics had to be prepared by Guild members, but this was not considered the most difficult part. When it came time for questions, especially difficult ones, the speakers had to be ready. Simple memorization of the truths of the faith was not sufficient; one had seriously to think the faith through and be prepared to defend it intelligently. In Westminster, Cardinal Bourne appointed priest directors to train Guild members in needed techniques. Of those directors, Doctor J. P. Arendzen stood out. Maisie Ward continues:

> Dr. Arendzen's lectures were the best possible; he not only knew theology at a depth and with a richness I have seldom seen equaled, he . . . could give us a dogma in modern English, making it accessible to us. . . . Born in Holland in 1873, he never lost his Dutch accent, yet it was he who first taught us to speak to the Englishman of today in an language he can understand.[9]

Classes were taken over two years; those for junior speakers looked at such topics as the idea of the visible Church, the

[8] Ward, *Unfinished Business*, 91.
[9] Ibid., 84.

Bible in the Church, the marks of the Church, the supremacy of the Holy Father, and papal infallibility. These were followed by a second part, which included the supernatural life, the Mystical Body of Christ, the Catholic moral system, our Lady, purgatory, and the externals of worship. In the second year, classes for the senior speakers were divided into three parts; in the first, faith and reason, revelation, internal and external evidence for the authenticity of the Gospels, the supernatural life, in-depth Christology, the Eucharist, and marriage were studied. This was followed by a concentration on the development of doctrine and the early heresies. The classes concluded with arguments for the existence of God, the problem of evil, free will and immortality. In addition to the core curriculum, lectures were offered on the use of Scripture and the lives of the saints. Also offered was technical training on how to relate a speech to the minds of listeners, how to develop ideas, the mental outlook necessary for a Catholic street-corner apologist, and practical advice on handling errors. Few college graduates would have had anything comparable, though a college education was hardly a criterion for acceptance into the Guild.

In its beginnings, the Guild was primarily concerned with defending the Church, and just as the Catholic Truth Society had strictly prohibited the attacking of other religious creeds in its pamphlets, so the Catholic Evidence Guild was equally clear that defense of Church teaching did not imply an all-out victory over those who held other theologies. Frank Sheed explained:

> One must never talk for victory—to show oneself right and the other man wrong. . . . If you talk for victory, sooner or later you will cheat. All polemic, religious, or other, is stained with cheating. You may not actually lie, but you will be

tempted to shade facts as might seem to weaken your case, soft-pedal them, divert the discussion away from them.... Whereas if your sole aim is to show what you hold, and what are its effects upon life as it is lived, there is no temptation to cheat; there is quite literally nothing to cheat about. You open your mind, you ask your hearers for their comments. You are not trying for a decision. The questions under discussion are too serious for that kind of quick settlement, their roots lie too deep in the person.[10]

The approach of the Guild as it presented the faith went from defense to proof to explanation. Ten years into its existence, it published its first *Training Outlines*. In the book's introduction, an explanation was given for the change of technique. The world of the mid-1920s and, in particular, the non-Catholic world of England, had moved from strong anti-Catholic prejudice to indifference. Previously, there had been a unified perception of what the Catholic Church opposed. Church doctrines invariably misconceived, but the apologists knew the misconceptions, refuted them convincingly, and held the attention of the crowd. Within a decade, all that changed:

Indifference lies over all such things. They have not come to deny the existence of God or the supremacy of Christ; they have simply turned their mind elsewhere. They are not sufficiently interested to doubt.... The Catholic then faces a crowd which is almost totally apathetic: it retains hostility to Catholicism, but a hostility from which all the sap is drained out. It is a hostility with vehemence and without shape—a slight discoloration marking the place of what was once a great wound.[11]

[10] Sheed, *The Church and I*, 64.
[11] Frank Sheed and Maisie Ward, *Catholic Evidence Training Outlines* (Ann Arbor, Mich.: Catholic Evidence Guild, 1992), 12.

Defense of the faith was no longer engaging nor, for that matter, was proof:

> Prove to a modern crowd that Our Lord instituted Confession—they will simply say, "What if He did?" Prove that He was God—they will say, "What if He was?" Prove that the Pope is not anti-Christ—they can but yawn and ask, "Who is, then?" [12]

The answer seemed to lie in explanation; showing what a doctrine means would be a speaker's principal occupation on the platform. To do this, one had to make contact with the crowd, keeping in mind the crowd was a collection of people conscious of no interest in anything the speaker might be likely to say. To capture their interest the Guild concluded that

> [h]uman beings as such find one thing interesting: they are interested in themselves. The Guild speaker, when he is building up a meeting—and indeed at all times—must be prepared to talk to the crowd about themselves. He must help them interpret their own lives and understand their own make-up. The key subject here, one of which the crowd never seems to weary, is the question of what man is made *for*. [13]

Man is made, of course, for the supernatural life, where can be found happiness with God. Once this had been explained, Catholicism as a way of life and as a totally integrated way of thought could be presented and explained as the very best means to achieving that supernatural life. The

[12] Ibid., 13.
[13] Ibid., 17.

Guild speakers delivered this message, despite the ever-present hecklers. On one occasion, a speaker was discussing our Lord's Ascension into heaven:

> Objector: If He'd gone up into the sky in Australia, He'd have been upside down.
> I: I can correct you on that. I've been up in the sky in Australia and I was not upside down.
> Objector: Ah, but you were in an airplane.[14]

Frank Sheed recalls:

> The truth is the hecklers were a kind of mirror in which occasionally we might catch a glimpse of ourselves. They were bigoted and prejudiced—what about us? Their one desire was to win the argument at all costs—so too often was ours. In the order of practicality, nothing was more useful in our outdoor life than being forced to consider bigotry and prejudice, in our hecklers, in ourselves.[15]

One of the reasons Guild preachers were as effective as they were was the spirituality given them in retreats, days of recollection, and at ordinary Guild meetings by the famous English Dominican Father Vincent McNabb. A realistic optimist, he believed hopelessness was the greatest crippler of humanity, and he tried to instill buoyancy into every faith-filled member's heart: "Someone once quoted, 'He who fights and runs away will live to fight another day.' 'No he won't,' said Father Vincent, 'he'll live to run away another day'".[16] A Jewish gentleman, Edward Siderman, a professional heckler

---

14 Sheed, *The Church and I*, 57.
15 Ibid.
16 Ward, *Unfinished Business*, 93.

for some forty years, wrote a book about Father McNabb; he titled it *A Saint in Hyde Park*.[17] His title speaks volumes about the priest's spirituality. Thank God Guild members had him. Thank God, too, the Church had, and still has, the Catholic Evidence Guild.

[17]Edward A. Siderman, *A Saint in Hyde Park: Memories of Father Vincent McNabb, O.P.* (Westminster, Md.: Newman Press, 1950).

XIII

The Maryknoll Bishops:
Francis X. Ford and James E. Walsh

On April 2, 1912, a twenty-year-old man from Cumber-land, Maryland, wrote to the Catholic Foreign Mission Society of America, more popularly known as Maryknoll. When the superiors who accepted him asked that he state his intentions, James Edward Walsh expressed sentiments shared by almost every man or woman religious who has ever served the foreign missions:

> I have read and been told about missionary work from my childhood, and always held it in high esteem, and the idea, I think I might say, just simply grew upon me. I made up my mind about a month ago. It does appeal to me more than working in this country for several reasons. I might add that I haven't a shadow of a doubt but that it is my vocation and I intend to see it through.[1]

The Society James E. Walsh and his six companions entered in 1912 had been established in Hawthorne, New York, the

[1] James Edward Walsh to Father James Anthony Walsh, April 2, 1912, cited in Robert E. Sheridan, M.M., *Bishop James E. Walsh As I Knew Him* (Ossining, N.Y.: Maryknoll Publications, 1981), 12.

previous year. Three days after their arrival, furniture began to be moved to the Society's new locale at Ossining, a mere five miles away. Some were brought by horse-drawn carriage; smaller pieces were taken in a Model T Ford. The site chosen was a hill, or knoll, dedicated to our Blessed Mother. Many years later, in response to the question if he were the first student officially to enter Maryknoll, James E. Walsh was quite clear: "No, Francis Ford arrived on September 14, the feast of the finding of the true cross. I reached Hawthorne on September 15, the seven dolors of the Blessed Mother." [2]

Both these men became Maryknoll priests, then later became bishops who defended the faith in China by their dry martyrdoms. Bishop Ford was buried on Chinese soil; Bishop Walsh was eventually released from prison and lived quietly, though very productively, at Maryknoll.

One of eight children, Francis X. Ford was born in Brooklyn, New York, in 1892. His father, Austin Ford, was a native of County Galway, Ireland. More than two decades before the Bishop's birth, the elder Ford, along with his brother Patrick, had begun a publication called *The Irish World* in New York City; Bishop Ford's mother, a native of Keokuk, Iowa, was among its contributors. The paper fiercely supported the cause of Irish independence and just as strongly defended the rights of the underprivileged. By nineteenth-century standards it was thought to be formidable journalism. Years later, when many in Maryknoll claimed Francis X. Ford their finest writer, he could legitimately claim an inherited ability.

[2] Ibid., 14.

The future missionary was a collegian at Cathedral College, Brooklyn, when the Catholic Foreign Mission Society was established. During those years, he heard a talk by one of Maryknoll's founders, Father James Anthony Walsh. The priest described the goals and purposes of the new community, emphasizing its spiritual vision. He stirred young Frank Ford's generous heart and gave him a confidence this was his vocation. Ford became the first seminarian admitted, and he was ordained to the priesthood in December 1917.

As a youngster, Ford had received a fine literary training at Saint Francis Prep in Brooklyn; by his college years he was an adept writer, and in the seminary his literary output was significant. When a contest was announced for a community song, his selection easily won. It was printed in *Field Afar*, the earliest Maryknoll magazine, and had as a melody the song *Maryland, My Maryland*, which was itself adapted from the German Christmas carol *O Tannenbaum*:

> To raise up sterling men for God
> Maryknoll, O Maryknoll,
> Whose blood may stain the heathen sod
> Maryknoll, fair Maryknoll,
> This is thy aim, thy sacred call,
> To bring Christ's name and grace to all.
> God speed them on to save man's soul,
> O House of God! My Maryknoll.
>
> O Mary, the Apostles' Queen
> For Maryknoll, thy Maryknoll,
> Throughout this country do thou glean,
> For Maryknoll, thy Maryknoll,
> Vocations to the darkened East,
> Who need the off'ring hand of Priest,

To bless them ere Death sounds its toll
From Maryknoll, thy Maryknoll.[3]

In 1918, one year after his ordination, Father Ford was a member of the first group of Maryknoll missionaries to go to China. There was nothing terribly surprising about this, as one biographer noted:

> It was common knowledge that Bishop Ford had a Chinese heart, even his eyes and his size blended well, that he was very pro-Chinese in his attitudes, what is [today] being termed acculturation. . . . All knew that his sympathies were with the underprivileged.[4]

He spent several months with Father Frederick Price, Maryknoll's co-founder, in Yeungkong and Kongmoon, both territories in southern China. In 1925, when the new southern China mission territory of Kaying was given to Maryknoll, Father Ford was one of the contingent who came to serve. Ten years later, on September 5, 1935, Bishop James Anthony Walsh, in his last public official act, consecrated Francis Ford as Bishop of Kaying, raising the mission territory to a vicariate. Bishop Ford remained there throughout the Second World War and opened an impressive minor seminary for the training of native Chinese clergy, dedicating himself tirelessly to the care of countless refugees who flooded the city of Kaying. During these years, too, he worked with the Maryknoll sisters in a way that had to be considered novel. Under the supervision of the Bishop and their superiors, teams

---

[3] Cited in Robert E. Sheridan, Compassion: A Vocational Autobiography with Background of Bishop Francis X. Ford, M.M. (Ossining, N.Y.: Maryknoll Publications, 1982), 5–6.
[4] Ibid., 7.

of sisters not only visited Chinese villages but took up residence in Chinese homes, catechizing the children, teaching the women, and instructing them so that they might be able to give a stronger religious fervor to their homes and families. After a certain amount of time, the sisters would return to their central mission station for rest and spiritual renewal. During these periods, Bishop Ford would often give them spiritual conferences, one of which has been put into book form with the title *Come Holy Spirit* (Orbis Books, 1976).

In 1946, as delegate of the priests in Kaying, the Bishop returned to the United States to attend the general chapter of Maryknoll. About the same time, no doubt reflecting on the nearly three decades he had spent in China and with an eye to the future, he composed this prayer:

> Grant us, Lord, to be the doorstep by which the multitudes may come to worship Thee. And if, in the saving of their souls, we are ground underfoot and spat upon and worn out, at least we shall have served Thee in some small way in helping pagan souls; we shall have become the King's Highway in pathless China.[5]

Such would soon be his own fate. In October 1949, the Chinese Nationalist forces of Chiang Kai-shek were defeated by those whom many Chinese felt to be merely agrarian reformers; in fact, the followers of Mao Tse-Tung were strong ideological Communists. With their victory, China became the totalitarian state it remains to this day. In early December 1950, the first of the Bishop's priests and sisters were imprisoned. The following April after a public trial, Bishop Ford and his secretary, Sister Joan Marie, were bound with

[5] Ibid.

ropes, placed under an escort of thirty armed soldiers, and taken to Canton prison. Sister Joan Marie was eventually released. Many years later she related an interesting incident to Bishop Fulton J. Sheen, who was then the national director of the Society for the Propagation of the Faith. Archbishop Sheen subsequently recounted it:

> The Bishop told Sister: "I am afraid the Communists are going to take over my property. Here is the key to my chapel; I want you to take out the Blessed Sacrament before It is desecrated." She took a loaf of bread and a key to the Bishop's chapel on the second floor of his home, removed the Blessed Sacrament and hid It in the loaf of bread. As she closed the chapel door, a Communist colonel who was known all over that part of China for his cruelty, said: "I am taking over possession of this chapel, I have a key." He tried to open the door, but it would not open. "Here, you open the door." She said: "I cannot; my hands are filled with bread." He said: "Give me the bread." She passed the bread to him and he looked down at it "as if it were an infant," she recalled, but he had his gun cocked all the while, as she opened the door. She removed the Blessed Sacrament to safety, and later on was imprisoned.[6]

As they were en route to prison, Bishop Ford reminded Sister Joan Marie and other Maryknoll sisters arrested at the same time that the Church is not only a triumphant Church but also a suffering one; they were to expect both joy and sorrow in their lives, but they were never to forget Christ was with them. As they were led from Kaying to Canton, they were spat on and stones were thrown at them. At one

---

[6] Fulton J. Sheen, *Treasure in Clay: The Autobiography of Fulton J. Sheen* (Garden City, N.Y.: Doubleday and Company, 1980; reprinted San Francisco: Ignatius Press, 1993), 116–17.

point, a banner was displayed that read: "The people's government welcomes the spy—Bishop Ford." [7]

Sister Joan Marie went on to tell Bishop Sheen: "[In prison] he was too weak to stand, so he leaned against a prison wall. His hair was long and white, and his beard matted, his face emaciated and pale from torture." [8] Despite his weakness somehow he secured bread and wine and celebrated Mass. Sister said going to Mass in a Gothic cathedral could not have meant nearly as much.

On the day of the death march, the Bishop was put in line between two other prisoners. The Chinese colonel who had seized the chapel tied a twenty-pound sack around the Bishop's neck. The Communists were not killing anyone outright, preferring instead for them to die a slow death. When Sister saw what was happening, she broke the line of march and shouted to the colonel to take a good look at the man. He ordered her back in line, but sometime later she noticed the Bishop was still marching, though the sack was no longer on his back. It had been taken off by the colonel, who put it on his own back; for doing so, the colonel was himself imprisoned and never heard from again. Sister always believed that the Communist colonel had done such a kind deed because he had once carried the Blessed Sacrament.

When Sister Joan Marie was finally released, it was she who brought the news to Maryknoll that Bishop Ford had died a dry martyr's death on February 21, 1952. A Chinese cook, whom the Bishop felt to be a faithful and loyal friend, betrayed him to the Chinese authorities. After the Bishop's death, the cook returned to the chapel, threw a rope around his neck, and committed suicide.

[7] Ibid., 117.
[8] Ibid.

Many biographies have been written about Bishop Ford; among the best are *Stone in the King's Highway* and *The Pagoda and the Cross*. Bishop Ford High School was named for him in Brooklyn; Bishop Fulton J. Sheen promoted his cause for beatification. One wonders, in light of Bishop Ford's own words, if he might have thought it too much fuss:

> I can see God's Kind Hand ... in overlooking all my baseness and placing me where I have but to imitate those about me to please Him. "I will go to the altar of God," I can truly say, "to God who giveth joy to my youth." My life ought to be one of prayer and praise and joy and thanks for God's kind mercies.[9]

James Edward Walsh was to have a different career than Bishop Ford in many ways. He would live sixty-six years as a priest and fifty-four as a bishop. He is remembered as the bishop who spent twelve years in a Communist prison, but by his fellow Maryknollers he was better known as the bishop who never uttered an unkind word about his captors:

> I have no bitterness toward those who tried and condemned me. I could just never feel angry with any Chinese. I felt that way almost from the first day I set foot in China in 1918, and it has grown stronger with the years, even during my imprisonment. I love the Chinese people.[10]

James Walsh was the second of nine children born to William and Mary Concannon Walsh. His grandparents were immigrants who had settled first in Parkersburg, West Virginia, before coming to Maryland. At nineteen, he graduated from

[9] Sheridan, *Compassion*, 20.
[10] Cited in James E. Walsh, M.M., *Description of a Missioner* (Ossining, N.Y.: Maryknoll Publications, 1976), 1.

Mount Saint Mary's College in Emmitsburg and then went to work for two years as a timekeeper in a steel mill. As soon as he heard about the Catholic Foreign Mission Society, he felt it was the life to which God called him. He became the second priest ordained for Maryknoll and three years later joined Fathers Price, Ford, and Bernard Meyer to comprise the first departure group for China. They left for Kwong Tung on the feast of our Lady's Nativity, September 8, 1918. One year later, after the death of Father Price, Father Walsh became the Superior General of the Maryknoll mission in China, acquiring the name Wha Lee Son (Pillar of Truth).

According to Father Walsh, the task of a missioner is to go to a place where he is not wanted but needed and to remain there until he is not needed but wanted. His career would prove this true. He once wrote that every missioner's duty "is to go to [a] place . . . to sell a pearl whose value, although of great price, is not recognized, to people who are determined not to accept it, even as a gift".[11]

More specifically related to China,

> [a missioner] must absorb a new and fascinating civilization, while eschewing its philosophy; he must adopt new viewpoints, while retaining old ones; he must learn and wield a new language, while clothing in it, not its own shopworn tags, but his own vigorous foreign thoughts. He must absorb not only the language itself, but whatever lies behind the language: the mentality that made it and is at once expressed and revealed, and even at times disguised by it. He must know and adopt many customs that are quite strange to him; . . . he finds himself obliged to maintain through life a flexibility of both mind and body that makes of him a perpetual gymnast.[12]

[11] Ibid., 3.
[12] Ibid., 3–4.

In 1927, Pope Pius XI appointed Father Walsh first bishop of the vicariate of Kongmoon. He was consecrated on Sancian Island, the site of Saint Francis Xavier's death centuries before.

The new Bishop looked upon his role as one of a servant, chosen to aid his fellow Maryknoll missionaries. He would remain in his diocese until 1936, when he returned to Maryknoll following the death of Bishop James Anthony Walsh. In April of that year, he was elected second Superior General of the Society and in the ensuing decade would supervise his community's first mission efforts in Latin America and Africa. A dozen years later, the Bishop returned to China at Rome's request. He became head of the Catholic Central Bureau in Shanghai, once again overseeing all missionary activity. Archbishop Sheen recalls:

> I flew into Peking, China, in 1948 with Bishop James E. Walsh of Maryknoll. Seated alongside him, I was reading Confucius, which prompted this remark: "I believe you and I are the only two missionaries in China who have read Confucius. We have to know the Chinese way of thinking. Before you can lead people to where you want them to be, you have to know where they are." As we landed he said, "I will never leave China unless I am put out." [13]

In 1949, Mao's Cultural Revolution was an accomplished fact, and it was generally believed the Church would suffer. Bishop Walsh's bureau was closed within two years, though he felt no compulsion whatever to leave a people he had grown to love. Maryknoll expressed serious concern for his safety, but it would be only a direct order from his superiors that would effect any change. For years he had been exhorting

[13] Sheen, *Treasure in Clay*, 115.

missionaries to remain at their posts, in imitation of Christ the Good Shepherd. He wrote an article in 1951 in *The China Missionary* listing seven reasons for Maryknollers (and, for that matter, all missionaries) to remain at their posts: (1) the wishes of the Church, (2) the desires of the Holy Father, (3) canonical responsibility, (4) the people the missionary was sent to serve, (5) China in general, (6) the missionary's vocation, and (7) the activity peculiar to the missionary's state in life.

It took seven years for the Communists finally to apprehend the Bishop, a delaying tactic, no doubt, to show the outside world that, at heart, Communism was not hostile to religion or religious leaders. His arrest came in 1958, and for the next two years incredible torture was to be his lot:

> He was subjected to constant questioning, any hour of the night, for short or long periods, and always underwent the agonizing endless repetition of the same questions. He was 67 at the time of his arrest; he had the courage to stand up to the questioning but after many months, his stamina was at low ebb. He had been sleeping on the open prison cement floors through all kinds of weather when he took ill. He was covered with boils that could not be treated in the primitive conditions in which he lived. It was almost a stroke of mercy that he was sentenced to 20 years, because then he was removed from this part of the prison and assigned to the hospital ward where his health was less threatened. For another ten years, what could he look forward to? [14]

For a brief time Bishop Walsh was allowed reading material, in particular, the classics of English literature. They were soon taken from him, however, and replaced with a loud

[14] Sheridan, *Bishop James E. Walsh*, 74.

radio outside his cell, which daily blasted some new line of Communist propaganda. Two things kept him sane: praying the Rosary, which he recited many times a day, and a Chinese-English dictionary. The Rosary was his spiritual "lifeline", and his study of the intricate characters of the Chinese language provided him countless hours of mental engagement.

The reason for Bishop Walsh's arrest was not apparent for some time. The Communists later explained that he had violated the law when he agreed to the request of a Chinese bishop to use his privilege of the British consular pouch to bring money from Hong Kong to help priests who were in dire financial straits. The Bishop never denied this at his trial; in fact, he felt the law unreasonable, imposing no obligation on him to obey it.

Through the years of his incarceration, some five thousand prisoners shared the same daily routine of physical exercise and listening to blaring radios. The Communists, for pragmatic reasons, took a certain amount of caution to ensure the health of the prisoners, as long as it suited their purposes. Packages sent through the Red Cross or Maryknoll were received, and not always opened. During his years in prison the Bishop received no outside news reports and had only one non-Chinese visitor, his brother, William C. Walsh, a former State Attorney General in Maryland, who was permitted a series of visits spread over several days in the summer of 1960.

Reflecting on this some years after the fact, Bishop Walsh had some interesting thoughts to share with a cloistered community of Visitation sisters in Wilmington, Delaware:

> I don't mind telling you that during my twelve years in prison, I was not unhappy a single day. I dreamed—well, first I woke up one morning and found myself in prison. I had been taken

the night before—handcuffed, surrounded by six guards. When I woke up the next morning I thought "This is what I've dreamed of—time to say all the prayers I couldn't say while I was working." . . . I had time to pray for my family, for my friends, for people all over the world, everybody under the sun. And I knew you were praying for me during those years. God put us here on earth to help each other. The best way to help people is to pray for them. . . . Prayer is so powerful. I am a living example of what prayer can do.[15]

On July 8, 1970, Bishop Walsh's life took a dramatic turn when he learned he was to be released (with no explanation given). He made his way by train to Canton, where he stayed overnight. He proceeded the next day to Hong Kong, where Maryknoll priests were waiting to greet him. In the Maryknoll sisters' hospital he received medical treatment and even offered Holy Mass for the first time in twelve years. An audience with Pope Paul VI followed soon after, in which the Holy Father had the opportunity to express the entire Church's gratitude to James Edward Walsh—and to praise the courageous witness of his defense of the faith. Sometime later, the Bishop met at the White House with President Richard M. Nixon, a long-standing foe of Communism, to report in detail on the nature of his treatment. What made the Bishop truly great has been well stated by one of his biographers:

> The secret of James E. Walsh, I feel, is not so much any particular combination of things he did, but rather, it is what he allowed God to do *to* him, and *through* him.
>
> Is this not the science of saints?[16]

---

[15] Cited in Sheridan, *Bishop James E. Walsh*, 77.
[16] Ibid., vi.

XIV

Jozsef Cardinal Mindszenty: The Dry Martyr of Hungary

Jozsef Mindszenty was born to Janos Pehm and his wife Bor-bala Kovacs on March 29, 1892. His surname comes from the town of his birth, Csehimindsent, in Vas County, Hun-gary. His father, a crop farmer who grew wine grapes on some twenty-five acres of land, would die a relatively young man. His mother, by contrast, lived to an old age and shared with her son many of the crosses and trials he was asked to endure. Both sides of the Mindszenty family had deep Hun-garian roots; they had lived through the Dual Monarchy of the Austro-Hungarian Empire. Although on paper a consti-tutional parliamentary state, Hungary was not, in fact, dem-ocratic. At the time of the First World War, only twenty-five percent of the adult male population were able to vote. The owners of great landed estates remained the unquestioned rulers and dominant class in Hungarian society. They were surrounded by landless peasants who comprised a large agrar-ian work force. It was this sort of culture that Mindszenty and his five siblings knew well in their childhood years.

The young Mindszenty was a hard-working student, conspicuous for his activity in the Catholic Youth Move-ment and the Marian Sodality. He entered the seminary upon graduation, was ordained to the priesthood in June 1915, and was assigned as a curate in a sizable parish:

> The priestly office was a source of profound joy to me. My instruction was well received, my sermons evoked response, and many believers came to Confession and Mass. I was especially happy when—even in cases of those who seemed to have hopelessly fallen out with God, the Church and themselves—I was able to revive faith by persuasion and guidance.[1]

This is not the statement of a proud man, but a humble man who allowed God to work through him. His humility, though, would be tested early on. Following his parish work he had been assigned to teach religion and Latin in a large gymnasium (a high school). These were the years following World War I, when Hungary was trying to establish itself as a republic, and the country was beset by left-wing revolutionaries who wanted to establish a Hungarian Soviet Republic. Early in 1919, young Father Mindszenty was asked to edit a newspaper in which he wrote articles sharply critical of Communist attempts to infiltrate the government:

> Throughout the country hostages were taken from among the opponents of the regime. I was one of them. In the middle of the night, a police inspector, accompanied by two patrolmen, pulled me out of bed and shouted in official tone and with official look, but in bad Hungarian, "You are under arrest." I replied that I had been so since February 9, 1919, and asked what this outlay of governmental authority was all about.[2]

---

[1] Jozsef Cardinal Mindszenty, *Memoirs* (New York: Macmillan Publishing, 1974), 3.
[2] Ibid., 6.

Father Mindszenty was threatened with expulsion and probably would have been expelled had the regime lasted. In fact, counter-revolutionaries, intending to restore the Habsburg monarchy, toppled the Soviet-backed attempt, though they were prevented by foreign pressure from restoring the King in person. In 1920, Hungary became, on paper, a monarchy; in reality it was a military dictatorship. Father Mindszenty did not leave his native country; instead, he quickly established a reputation as a solid thinker, a holy priest, and a hard worker. There followed the interim period between world wars, but by the forties yet another dictator had emerged on the world scene. Hitler and the Nazis gained power and began their campaign of Jewish extermination.

In early 1944, Bishop Janos Mikes, one of Hungary's best-known prelates, brought Jozsef Mindszenty to the attention of the Papal Nuncio. As a result, Pope Pius XII appointed him Bishop of Veszprem. In the summer of 1944, Jews living in Budapest were ordered to live in ghettos. Bishop Mindszenty and his episcopal colleagues lost no time in responding:

> When innate rights, such as the right to life, human dignity, personal freedom, the free exercise of religion, freedom of work, livelihood, property, etc., or rights acquired by legal means, are unjustly prejudiced either by individuals, by associations, or even by the representatives of the government, the Hungarian Bishops, as is their duty, raise their protesting voices and point out that these rights are conferred not by individuals, not by associations, not even by representatives of the government, but by God Himself.... These rights cannot be taken away by any person [or] any earthly power.[3]

---

[3] Cited in Mindszenty, *Memoirs*, 14–15.

The bishops' protest was ignored, of course. Posters began to be hung on churches, announcing that services would be held in thanksgiving for the successful liberation of the city of Veszprem from the Jews. The Bishop protested vigorously and insisted that no Masses be said, no *Te Deum*s be sung and no services of any sort be conducted while such offensive posters were on public display. His action hardly went unnoticed:

> A statement was issued to the effect that I had been arrested because I offered resistance to the authorities and their decisions, and to government officials, and because I tried to organize a protest march in order to incite the populace to violence. Public order and safety had been gravely endangered by my actions.[4]

The Bishop was imprisoned this second time for firmly held principles. During his incarceration, many events he had foreseen—destruction of cities, halting of transportation, closure of mail and telephone systems—became realities. The Russian Communist "liberators" were marching through Hungary, and although the Bishop was able to return to his home in safety, he had no misconceptions about their purpose. At first, they tried to show their best colors; in October 1944, the Russian high command encouraged all citizens to carry on their work peaceably, with every assurance religion would not be interfered with. Bishop Mindszenty took their words to mean that the public celebration of Mass would continue, while the social, cultural, or charitable works of the Church would quickly halt. In Budapest, Cardinal Primate Seredi strongly influenced Catholic opinion, both clerical and lay; he admonished priests to remain at their

[4] Ibid., 18.

assignments, even if it meant martyrdom. To the laity, his message was steadfastness in the faith. Such impact had Communist authorities seriously worried. On August 20, 1945, in Budapest, there was an unmistakable repudiation of Communism by Hungarian Catholics. Bishop Mindszenty remembered:

> On that day five hundred thousand believers followed the uncorrupted right hand of Saint Stephen, while hundreds of thousands lined the route of the procession. Budapest was declaring in a thunderous voice: the most precious possession of our nation is the heritage that the sainted King has left behind. Therefore we stand fast by Christianity and are not going to make a home in our country for atheism and materialism.[5]

By 1945 the Communists had made significant inroads in Hungary; one of the ways they did this was by actively participating in Catholic events, hoping to prove they were religious people at heart. While individual Communists were ingratiating themselves, the government was legislating an end to catechetical instruction for children and allowing no more than two Catholic newspapers to be published, citing a paper shortage as their reason. Morality also suffered; separation was now sufficient grounds for divorce, even if the couple themselves did not bring about the separation. As Hungary moved toward more secularization, it also suffered a loss of political freedom, with a restriction on the formation and activity of political parties.

On September 8, 1945, Cardinal Mindszenty learned from the President of the Hungarian Episcopal Conference that Pope Pius XII wanted him to take over the Archdiocese of

[5] Ibid., 31.

Esztergom, making him the Primate of Hungary. He asked for twenty-four hours before he accepted:

> When I gave my consent, I was trusting wholeheartedly in our people, brave defenders of their faith who had so often and so movingly proved their attachment to Christianity. But I confess that I was also hoping somewhat to obtain support from the Allied Control Commission, which after the Armistice became the supreme authority and highest power in our defeated nation. Representatives of the military missions of the Western Powers sat on this commission alongside the Russians.[6]

When Communist control was a reality, occupying forces said they would allow a power-sharing agreement in which the people's party, or shareholders, would actively participate in government. This was aimed at world opinion because Communist tactics of intimidation toward their political adversaries became so pronounced; there was, in fact, no power sharing. Cardinal Mindszenty knew well the challenges he faced:

> In Christian circles, Marxist tenets gain a foothold only when ... religion has lost its place as a determinant force in social life. It is well known that people who have become uncertain about their beliefs will be on the lookout for new and stronger premises. In such cases, Marxism seems like salvation. The waverer hopes that dialectical materialism will supply the answers to those questions religion and metaphysics leave as mysteries and do not answer.[7]

With this in mind, the Cardinal announced plans to intensify the religious life of the entire nation. A campaign of

[6] Ibid., 33.
[7] Ibid., 45–46.

prayer and penance was undertaken in all the dioceses of Hungary, which was so successful it attracted a large number of non-Catholics. It seemed the Hungarian people were prepared to take a heavy cross upon themselves, much as Christ did, and to carry it in union with him. In a powerful sermon preached in a church in Budapest in February 1946, the Cardinal said:

> Only a praying humanity can build a better world. I am not now thinking merely of such external things as houses, bridges, streets, cables, and the like, but I am thinking of relations with our fellow men and with our own inner selves. We must fit into our planning and our building, self-sacrificing enthusiasm and the power of prayer. Prayer can intensify physical and spiritual forces; it is a power that can even overcome the laws of nature.[8]

From that point on, the Cardinal was surely a marked man. In 1948, the Church in Hungary celebrated the tenth anniversary of the International Eucharistic Congress held in Budapest. This was followed a month later by a large procession in honor of Our Lady of Fatima. The government indirectly interfered with these events by refusing to run more than two trains a day. In addition, they stepped up their campaign against the Cardinal: "We will annihilate Mindszentyism! The well being of the Hungarian people and peace between church and state depend on it."[9]

They launched a press campaign against him, alleging his cruelty to the people. School children and factory workers were ordered into the streets to demonstrate against the Primate; it was made to appear that his own bishops opposed

[8] Cited in Mindszenty, *Memoirs*, 47.
[9] Ibid., 83–84.

him and wanted him removed from office. Petitions began to appear in offices, and individuals were forced to sign their names demanding Mindszenty's resignation. In time the Cardinal's secretary was arrested, and he knew it would not be long before he was taken.

As the Cardinal related it, his arrest occurred on the eve of the feast of Saint Stephen, the first martyr. Communist agents came to his residence in Esztergom and lost no time:

> They drove into the yard and turned their whole column of cars around, ready for instant departure. They noisily trampled into the house, and with thudding boots approached my apartment on the first floor. I was kneeling on the prie-dieu, praying and meditating. The door flew open. [Police colonel] Desci entered. In a state of high agitation he confronted me and declared: "We have come to arrest you." Eight or ten police officers thronged after him into the room. I was surrounded by them. When I demanded that they show the warrant for arrest, they brawled brashly: "We don't need anything like that." One of them added that the democratic police were alert and could find traitors, spies, and currency smugglers even when they wore a Cardinal's robes.[10]

He was taken to 60 Andrassy Street in Budapest: "Here Hungarians who had been taught their trade by Hitler's Gestapo had already created, during the period of German occupation, a gruesome place of torture, a true center of terror."[11]

Cardinal Mindszenty would be treated in no different fashion. He was subjected to the grossest personal humiliation; he was stripped, brainwashed, tortured, and interrogated countless times with the same questions. Authorities wanted

[10] Ibid., 89.
[11] Ibid., 90.

to know when he had become an enemy of the state. He replied that to the best of his knowledge the Hungarian people did not consider him such an enemy. Why, they asked, did he persist in opposing progress? The Cardinal said that he had never hindered true progress, but when he observed what had happened to his country since the Communist takeover, he failed to see how any of it could be defined as progress. Finally, he was accused of consorting with the United States' "imperialists". That was true, Mindszenty observed; he had indeed opened communication with the Americans when his own Hungarian government refused to oppose the constant infringements by the Soviet occupying forces.

The charges brought against the Cardinal were so ludicrous as to appear bizarre. In addition to his opposition to the founding of the republic, he was accused of secretly conspiring with Otto von Habsburg in 1947 and preventing the crown of Saint Stephen from being returned to Hungary so that he might ensure von Habsburg's right to the Hungarian throne and crown him with the crown of Saint Stephen at the appropriate time. Finally, his contacts with the United States, it was said, were made for the sole purpose of inciting a third world war. Again and again the Cardinal was asked to sign a declaration attesting to the veracity of these charges, but to no avail. With each refusal, he was returned to his cell.

Cardinal Mindszenty was brought to trial in February 1949. The prosecution's case rested on three points: (1) he had led an organization that was planning to overthrow the government; (2) he had engaged in espionage against the Hungarian state; and (3) he had illegally used foreign currencies. His trial was little more than an exercise in Communist propaganda, and for all he knew, his sentence of life imprisonment would be the last word. Once in prison, his day consisted of

rising at five o'clock in the morning, chores at six, and breakfast at seven. From eight in the morning till four in the afternoon, one simply waited for the opportunity to go outside
for a walk. The only deviation from this monotony was lunch
at one o'clock and dinner at six; lights were expected to be
out by nine in the evening. After nine months, the Cardinal
was permitted to offer Mass, though not frequently. Also, he
was allowed to borrow one book per week from the prison
library. A legitimate question to be raised is how one copes
with such a routine. For Cardinal Mindszenty, much of the
answer was to be found in a life of prayer:

> A stay in prison can direct men's minds towards God. Soli-
> tude often revives memories of long forgotten religious truths.
> Even lukewarm Christians and people indifferent to religion
> who have forgotten how to pray, and no longer perceive the
> needs of their souls and who have neglected the command-
> ment to keep the Lord's day holy, are reunited with their
> Creator by attendance at the prison chapel, perhaps forever
> after.[12]

The periods of solitude could indeed be beneficial, but prison
existence was anything but normal:

> My religious life certainly suffered from my surroundings,
> but it was not destroyed. There was a great deal I lacked that
> I had earlier possessed, but many of my religious exercises
> became all the more intensive. I also missed weekly confes-
> sion; in place of it I practiced detailed probing of my con-
> science twice a day. I regularly held novenas and triduums. I
> prayed daily to my guardian angel, St. Joseph, and to the
> saints of an easy death, the apostles John and Judas Thad-
> deus. I also prayed to the saint of the Little Way, Thérèse of

[12] Ibid., 163.

Lisieux, who has rained a shower of roses upon earth, to the saints of each day, and to my twin brother who had died in childhood. . . . I included the concerns of the entire world in my rosary prayers. . . . Every day I prayed six rosaries.[13]

Events contributing to the Cardinal's final release from prison were political. Agitation for more political freedom had been mounting in eastern Europe in the early fifties. Such forces had experienced a bit of success in Poland with the October Revolution of 1956. Collectivization of farms ended, police terror was checked, and a freer political and intellectual climate came about. It is not at all surprising Hungary would have followed suit:

The moderate minded Communist leader Imre Nagy, who had tried to liberalize the Hungarian regime from 1953 to 1955, but had been dismissed, now returned to power. He undertook a policy of liberal concessions, even freeing political prisoners like Cardinal Mindszenty, but the very concessions increased the revolutionary pressures from workers and students who once again rioted in the streets of Budapest, and threatened to drive out the Communist regime, restore parliamentary government, and cut the ties with Moscow. Kruschev, thereupon, dispatched an army of tanks and artillery and forcefully reestablished Communist rule. The revolt was suppressed. . . . Two years later Nagy himself was executed. . . . The open show of force by Moscow in Budapest destroyed illusions about the benevolence and liberality of Stalin's successors and shook the faithful in Western Europe and elsewhere.[14]

[13] Ibid., 165–66.
[14] R. R. Palmer and Joel Colton, *A History of the Modern World* (New York: Alfred A. Knopf, 1965), 854.

From the morning of October 31, 1956, Cardinal Mindszenty carried on official duties, including a radio address in
Parliament, until the evening of November 3, when he was
once again in exile:

> I clambered aboard the saving deck of the American Em-
> bassy to escape being carried off to the Soviet Union and to
> wait for the day that would once more permit me to work in
> behalf of my native land.[15]

President Dwight D. Eisenhower gladly gave permission for
the Cardinal to take up residence at the embassy, where
every possible courtesy was extended to him. Because of the
efforts of Cardinal Francis Spellman in New York, the National Catholic Welfare Conference paid one thousand dol-
lars annually toward his keep, so that no criticism could be
raised in the United States about a Catholic priest being provided for indefinitely. He would remain in the embassy fifteen years, never leaving day or night. A good part of these
years were taken up with the writing of his memoirs and
serving the Catholic people who worked on the embassy
staff. He often commented on the unusually devout Catholics he encountered there; in addition, he won the friendship and respect of those of other faiths who were his official
hosts.

During the Nixon era of détente with the Communist
world, the climate had changed drastically. It became much
easier for the Cardinal to leave the embassy, allowing him to
travel to many parts of the world to lecture on his experiences; he eventually took up official residence at a seminary
in Vienna, where he would spend the remainder of his life.
Before doing any of this, his first stop in September 1971

---

[15] Mindszenty, *Memoirs*, 212.

after his release was Vatican City, where he received an audience with Pope Paul VI. Embracing him, the Holy Father took his pectoral cross and hung it around the Cardinal's shoulders and then invited him to concelebrate at the opening Mass of an episcopal synod. In his sermon, Pope Paul expressed the gratitude of the entire Church for this fighter for freedom and defender of the faith:

> He is a guest whom We have awaited with longing ... a glorious symbol of the unity between the Hungarian Church and the Apostolic See, a unity that has existed for a thousand years ... a symbol of unspeakable strength rooted in faith, and in selfless devotion to the church. He has proved this first of all by his tireless activity and alert love, then by prayer and long suffering. Let us praise the Lord and together say a reverent, cordial *Ave* to this exiled and highly honored archbishop.[16]

His defense of the faith is not forgotten. In the twenty-first century, hundreds and thousands still come annually to the Cardinal's tomb in the cathedral of Esztergom to pray and to remember.

---

[16] Cited in Mindszenty, *Memoirs*, 237.

XV

With God in Russia:
The Story of Father Walter Ciszek, S.J.

The late Archbishop Fulton J. Sheen once said if you ever want to know God more intimately, speak to those who are holy or those who have suffered. In the person of Jesuit Father Walter Ciszek, we find both sanctity and suffering. Twenty-three years behind the iron curtain give one a unique perspective on holiness, not to mention suffering. It also provides one a unique vantage point to speak of the ways of God:

> God has a special purpose, a special love, a special providence for all those he has created. God cares for each of us.... The circumstances of each day of our lives, of every moment of every day, are provided for us by him.... But maybe we are all just a little afraid to accept [this truth] in all its shattering simplicity, for its consequences in our lives are both terrible and wonderful.[1]

Father Walter Ciszek might be described as one who defended the faith by steadfastness and trust in God. Born to

---

[1] Walter J. Ciszek, S.J., with Daniel Flaherty, S.J., *He Leadeth Me* (San Francisco: Ignatius Press, 1995), 201.

Polish immigrant parents in Shenandoah, Pennsylvania, on November 4, 1904, he attended Saint Casmir's parish and parochial school. His parents had settled in this coal-mining town in the 1890s; his father, a miner, gave him his toughness, while his mother bequeathed him a strong Catholic faith:

> I was a bully, the leader of a gang, a street fighter—and most of the fights I picked on purpose, just for devilment. I had no use for school, except insofar as it had a playground where I could fight or wrestle or play sports—any sport.[2]

Be that as it may, by the time he had finished eighth grade, he had made up his mind he wanted to become a priest: "My father refused to believe it. Priests, in his eyes, were holy men of God; I was anything but that."[3]

At the time, many young students of Polish descent studied at Ss. Cyril and Methodius Seminary in Orchard Lake, Michigan. During Walter's first year there, he became enormously interested in the Jesuits after reading a biography of Saint Stanislaus Kostka. He admired the tenacity of the saint, who walked from Warsaw to Rome to join the Jesuits. He also sympathized with the young man's plight; he encountered much family opposition when he announced his desire to enter the Society of Jesus. Walter would face much the same from his own father, who wanted him to complete his studies at Orchard Lake. Nonetheless, in September 1928, he entered Saint Andrew's-on-Hudson at Poughkeepsie, New York. His life as a Jesuit had begun.

---

[2] Walter J. Ciszek, S.J., with Daniel Flaherty, S.J., *With God in Russia* (San Francisco: Ignatius Press, 1997), 18.
[3] Ibid., 20.

A future in the Soviet Union was far removed from the young man's mind, but in the late twenties, Pope Pius XI was very much interested in sending priests to Russia. Ten years earlier the Communists had assumed power, causing the Church to face intense persecution; Catholics and Orthodox were not allowed to practice their faith publicly, seminaries were closed, clerics imprisoned, and churches were turned into museums. With this bearing on his mind, the Holy Father addressed a letter "to all seminarians, especially our Jesuit sons", explaining the new center of studies to be opened in Rome for the training of men for the Russian mission and encouraging priestly candidates to consider prayerfully the papal request. The idea was never out of Walter Ciszek's mind as he went to the Juniorate of the Jesuits in Wernersville, Pennsylvania, for the study of the humanities and later to Woodstock College in Maryland for philosophy. In 1934, theological studies in Rome followed and the fulfillment of what by now had become a dream—assignment to the Russian mission:

> Like all the Jesuit students of theology in Rome, I lived at the old Collegio Santo Roberto Bellarmino on the Via del Seminario and studied theology at the Gregorian University just off the Piazza Pilotta. At the same time, I was studying the Russian language, liturgy, and history in the Collegio Russico, or Russicum, on the Via Carlo Cattaneo, not far from the basilica of St. Mary Major.[4]

Father Ciszek was ordained to the priesthood in June 1937, with faculties to offer Mass in the Eastern rite and the privilege of offering in the Roman rite, should the necessity arise. As a newly ordained priest, he was disappointed to learn he

---

[4] Ibid., 28.

was unable to go immediately to Russia. Instead, his Jesuit superior assigned him to Albertyn, Poland, where the need for priests was great. He would function in a parish as well as teach Ethics to younger Jesuits studying at the Oriental Rite Mission. It was very fulfilling and he enjoyed it greatly.

His Russian opportunity would finally arrive in September 1939, though the circumstances bringing it about were anything but favorable. Hitler invaded Poland; German troops quickly surrounded Warsaw and the city was bombarded. The devastated Polish army began moving in an easterly direction, and no communication could be made with Warsaw radio. People seemed to sense Poland's fate. Since Father Ciszek was American born, in the interest of safety he was temporarily made superior of the Jesuit mission in Albertyn. He and a fellow Jesuit were finally able to leave the country the following spring, on the Feast of Saint Joseph, March 19, 1940. For their trip to Russia, Father Ciszek secured a Polish passport, since it would have been extremely difficult to enter with an American one. The two priests created new identities as working men desiring to work for the Russians in the Ural Mountains: "I became 'Wladimir Lypinski', a Pole and a widower, whose family had been killed in a German air raid." [5]

The priests shared the long, tedious train ride with many Polish Jews fleeing Hitler's soldiers. After arriving in the Urals, Father Ciszek got a job at a lumber camp, and after some months began driving a truck at the same camp. The people quickly discovered he was a priest, and they were delighted to have Mass offered for them and to have their children baptized. He greatly admired the risks so many of these

---

[5] Ibid., 44.

people took to assist at his clandestine Masses. He admired, too, their deep Catholic faith:

> I found the teenagers, especially, interested in religion. They had heard it discussed and ridiculed so much in school they wanted to know more. Under the pretext of picking mushrooms or huckleberries, we would arrange meetings in the forest after work at night. There, behind a hillock, or in some sunken spot, we would talk for hours about God and man's relation to God and his fellow man. They were full of questions, eager to learn. Yet, at the end of such a session, they would make me promise not to tell anyone what we had talked about, and we would return to camp by different paths.[6]

The friendships he formed with many of these people lasted little more than one year. Then at three o'clock in the morning one day in June 1941, the Soviet secret police invaded the lumber camp and began searching for any type of contraband. They discovered a bottle of wine (used at Mass), tooth powder, cotton, and some papers on which a little child had been practicing the alphabet; all were immediately construed as elements to be used to blow up the camp. Father Ciszek and the others were held at gunpoint; he was eventually taken to a juvenile home at Chusovoy, then to prison at Perm. In the prison he was subjected to a form of interrogation that would have made lesser men despair:

> Sometimes I'd be called out twice a day, sometimes not at all. The sessions might last anywhere from an hour to all day. The questions were always the same. Sometimes I'd have to sit bolt upright on the edge of a chair for hour after hour, and sometimes, if the interrogator didn't like an answer, he'd

[6] Ibid., 58.

give me a blow on the face that would send me sprawling on the floor.

Two or three times in the months I was at Perm, the interrogator summoned a pair of guards and led me into an adjoining room with thick carpets on the floor and heavily padded walls. There I would be worked over with rubber clubs on the back of the head, and when I'd try to drop my head, I'd get a smashing blow to the face. . . .

Several times, too, . . . I was put in a small, black room like a box, so pitch dark I literally couldn't see my hand in front of my face, and stifling hot. I might be there an hour or overnight. I was told to think over the questions and my answers, and decide whether or not I might be able to remember a few more details of the "truth".[7]

His interrogators obviously had many sources of information; they knew they were questioning a United States' citizen, a Catholic priest, and a Roman-trained member of the Society of Jesus who had used a Polish passport to enter Russia. Somehow they sensed Vatican involvement and were relentless in their probing. When all failed, they transferred Father Ciszek from Perm to the infamous Lubianka prison, in the heart of Moscow. It had once been headquarters for the KGB, which was and still is an imposing, formidable structure. Father Ciszek's train ride to Moscow was memorable in at least one way:

I propped my head against the window frame as if I were asleep and began to pray. This sort of mental prayer was what had kept me going until now; by means of it, I never lost courage. . . . It reminded me of my reasons for being here, of my resolve, no matter what the consequences, to do whatever I did only for God. He would sustain me. This thought—

---

[7] Ibid., 69–70.

that no matter how lonely I was, I was never really alone—gave me courage again now.[8]

A quarter-pound of bread, a cube and a half of sugar, and a cup of boiling water hardly seems like a meal worth waiting for; not so if one is a prisoner at Lubianka. Compared to previous treatment, this was a welcome relief. In addition, Lubianka was neat, clean, and also spacious since it had once been a hotel. Lunch was at noon, supper at six o'clock. Aside from this routine, the only change was a guard's supervising of each prisoner's going to showers and baths. After one year of this solitary confinement, Walter Ciszek was sentenced to fifteen years at hard labor in Siberia. The official who had pronounced the sentence asked the prisoner if he were content with the verdict:

> "I really don't have much choice, do I?" I said. They both found that uproariously funny. Then the commissar said, "You're getting off easy, you know." Since I had "no complaint", he told me to sign the document ... According to the date on the "verdict" I had signed, it was July 26, 1942.[9]

What Father Ciszek did not know was that four more years would elapse before his hard labor would begin. During these years, he was given liberal access to the prison's library; he referred to these years as the ones in which he obtained his "doctorate" from "Lubianka University". Classics of Russian literature were available to him—particularly the works of Tolstoy and those of Dostoyevsky, Turgenev, Gogol, and Leskov—as well as those of Jack London, Charles Dickens, Shakespeare, Goethe, and Schiller. He was determined the

[8] Ibid., 73.
[9] Ibid., 125.

prison routine would not get him down, and continuous reading helped greatly. More importantly, daily spiritual routine kept him not only sane but very connected to his loving Creator:

> After breakfast, I would say Mass by heart—that is, I would say all the prayers, for of course I couldn't actually celebrate the Holy Sacrifice. I said the Angelus morning, noon, and night as the Kremlin clock chimed the hours. Before dinner, I would make my noon *examen* (examination of conscience); before going to bed at night I'd make the evening *examen* and points for the morning meditation, following Saint Ignatius' *Spiritual Exercises*.
>
> Every afternoon, I said three rosaries—one in Polish, one in Latin, and one in Russian—as a substitute for my breviary. After supper, I spent the evening reciting prayers and hymns from memory or even chanting them out loud: the *Anima Christi*, the *Veni Creator*, the *Salve Regina*, the *Veni, Sancte Spiritus*, especially the *Dies Irae* and the *Miserere*—all the things we had memorized in the novitiate as novices, the hymns we had sung during my years in the Society, the prayers I had learned as a boy back home.[10]

In addition to his daily spiritual and mental regime, he included forty-five minutes of calisthenics to keep his body as active as his mind. All these activities provided him solace in the midst of his suffering. In later years, his experience caused him to look more closely at the mystery of suffering:

> [W]hy the passion? Why pain and suffering? Is God so vindictive that he must inflict pain and suffering on those who follow him? The answer lies not in God's will but in the world in which we live and try to follow his will. Christ's

[10] Ibid., 88.

life and suffering were redemptive; his "apostolate" in the scheme of salvation was to restore the original order and harmony in all creation that had been destroyed by sin.... But Christ's redemptive act did not of itself restore all things; it simply made the work of redemption possible, it began our redemption.... It is not the Father, not God, who inflicts suffering upon us but rather the unredeemed world in which we must labor to do his will, the world in whose redemption we must share.[11]

In an even more poignant vein, Father Ciszek continues:

This simple truth, that the sole purpose of man's life on earth is to do the will of God, contains in it riches and resources enough for a lifetime. Once you have learned to live with it uppermost in mind, to see each day and each day's activities in its light, it becomes more than a source of eternal salvation; it becomes a source of joy and happiness here on earth. The notion that the human will, when united with the divine will, can play a part in Christ's work of redeeming all mankind is overpowering.[12]

These had to have been sustaining thoughts as this holy man made his way to Siberia, north of the Arctic Circle, to work in a slave labor camp.

When Father Ciszek arrived in Siberia the climate was itself a culture shock; it was so frigid that many of the prisoners remained awake and paced throughout the first night to keep their blood circulating. The howling wind seemed to intensify with each passing hour. Those who did lie down arose with great physical difficulty at six in the morning to be given six hundred grams of bread and ten grams of sugar,

---

[11] Ciszek, *He Leadeth Me*, 116.
[12] Ibid., 117.

rations to last the entire day. In his famous memoir, *With God in Russia*, Father Ciszek describes the prisoners' day, which began at sunrise and continued well beyond sunset. They were taken to nearby docks where huge amounts of coal were to be shoveled onto conveyor belts and finally onto ships, which would export it. All day long coal was brought from the area's coal mines, piled up, and shoveled on. The prisoners were given a daily quota, which had to be met before they were allowed to return home. The river in this part of Siberia, called Dudinka, was navigable only a few months of the year, so the ships had to be loaded with tremendous speed. Father Ciszek describes being sent into the cold, dusty hold of the ship late in the afternoon following many hours of loading coal; it had to be spread around so more coal could be loaded. As they worked to scatter it, coal still kept pouring down the conveyor belt:

> As the hold filled up, the danger increased. There was no room to move, and there was more chance you might slip on the shifting piles of coal and fall into the path of the chunks roaring down the chute. When it finally got too bad, we would shout as loud as we could and bang on the deck with our shovels. The belt would stop for a minute, we'd scramble out, then continue distributing the coal from the hatchway. There were a lot of injuries on this job, and everyone hated it. But the work schedule had to be met; we were expendable.[13]

With the exception of one half-hour for lunch, during which the prisoners ate a portion of the bread left over from their breakfast ration, this was their daily existence, with no deviation. One could only imagine the solace the Holy Sacrifice

[13] Ciszek, *With God in Russia*, 206.

of the Mass brought to Father Ciszek and a fellow prisoner
as they secretly offered it in the barracks after their day's work.
It brought great joy, too, to those who attended—the fellow
prisoners, who made wine from raisins and bread out of flour
they managed to secure from the kitchen.

> You cannot explain all of this, I know, to those who do not
> believe.... Yet what a source of sustenance it was to us then,
> how much it meant to us to have the Body and Blood of
> Christ as the food of our spiritual lives in this sacrament of
> love and joy. The experience was very real; you could feel its
> effects upon your mind and heart.... These men, with sim-
> ple and direct faith, grasped this truth and they believed in
> it. They could not explain it as a theologian might, but they
> accepted it and they lived by it and were willing to make
> voluntary sacrifices even in a life of almost total deprivation,
> in order to receive the bread of life.[14]

Wherever Father Ciszek went, it became known very quickly
he was a priest. People sought him out, sometimes for coun-
sel, sometimes for mere conversation. Most often, though, it
was to have their sins forgiven in Confession. He became
enormously impressed with the faith of those who believed
in the Holy Eucharist and the sacrifices they would make to
assist at Mass. The saintly Jesuit began to realize more and
more his own human instrumentality; God was truly at work
in this entire process, and Walter Ciszek was the vehicle he
was using to bring so many to himself through the sacraments of his Church:

> To realize this was a matter of joy and humility. You realized
> that they came to you as a man of God ... a man chosen
> from among men and ordained from men in the things that

---

[14] Ciszek, *He Leadeth Me*, 125 and 132.

are of God; you realized, too, that this imposed upon you an obligation of service . . . with no thought of personal inconvenience, no matter how tired you might be physically or what risks you might be running in the face of official threats.[15]

The farther north one travels in Siberia, the more intensely cold it becomes. Zapadwaya, one of the oldest mines in the region, was his next stop. He was forced to be in the company of many rough, criminal types, in an area where accumulation of snow often exceeded a person's height and vision and the wind was relentless as it continually changed directions. Father Ciszek and his fellow prisoners worked ten-hour days with no lunch break in a wet, damp mine. On certain days when the weather became so intense the prisoners could not work, they would be taken on horse-drawn carts to the mine to make preparations for the next day's work. Father Ciszek remained here for one year, during which he witnessed the death of seven miners who were killed instantly in a blast in a restricted area with poor ventilation. The episode caused him to think about the death that awaits all of us, regardless of the circumstances:

[T]he thought of death itself does not terrify me, had not terrified me all through the war, or prison, or the prison camps. Death must come to all men at the end of this earthly life, but it is not therefore evil. If the good news of Christianity is anything, it is this: that death has no hidden terror, has no mystery, is not something man must fear. It is not the end of life, of the soul, of the person. Christ's death on Calvary was not in itself the central act of salvation, but his death and *resurrection*; it was the resurrection that completed his

15 Ibid., 108.

victory over sin and death, the heritage of man's original sin that made a Redeemer and redemption necessary. This was the "good news" of salvation, meant to remove mankind's last doubts, last fears, about the nature of death.[16]

Three months short of the completion of his prison sentence, Father Ciszek was freed. But, he could not leave the Soviet Union, and before he traveled he had to report to local authorities—a limited freedom, but freedom nonetheless. His freedom came about through the intervention of a Lithuanian medical doctor named Janos from the medical center at Kayerkhan. Janos, a devout Catholic, had met and examined Father Ciszek in the spring of 1955, concluding that any further work in the mines would hasten Father Ciszek's death. He therefore recommended the priest's immediate release; when prison authorities procrastinated, he became irate, threatening to submit a full report and blame the camp's resident doctor in the event of Father Ciszek's death. Immediately, the priest was taken out of the mines and assigned to work in the stables, cleaning and feeding the horses. In early April 1955, Father Ciszek's restricted freedom followed:

> I was so self-conscious, I didn't know how to walk like a free man. My arms dangling at my sides rather than folded behind my back, felt strange.... There was a train at the station. I boarded it, and no one paid the slightest attention to me. I couldn't believe it. It seemed like a movie, as if everything were just a series of pictures unrolling before my eyes, or as if I were in a dream and might wake up at any moment.[17]

[16] Ibid., 145.
[17] Ciszek, *With God in Russia*, 316.

Finally, in 1963, Father Ciszek left Russia. He and another American were exchanged for a Russian couple being held for espionage in the United States. After returning to his native land, he became a member of the John XXIII Center for Eastern Christian Studies at Fordham University, New York City. In addition to writing *With God in Russia*, he further explored the spiritual dimensions of his journey in a second book, *He Leadeth Me*. Father Ciszek became an internationally known director of the Ignatian Spiritual Exercises and led countless people in their search for God and his plan for their lives. He died at the center in which he worked, appropriately enough, on the Feast of the Immaculate Conception, December 8, 1984, and is buried at the Jesuit cemetery in Wernersville, Pennsylvania.

It has been said that in his later years his counseling and retreat work were marked by a simplicity in method and a humility of heart that attracted all sorts and varieties of people to him. In part, it was due to his complete abandonment to God, learned over a score of years in the Soviet Union:

> I was brought to make this perfect act of faith, this act of complete self-abandonment to his will, of total trust in his love and concern for me and his desire to sustain and protect me.... I knew I could no longer trust myself, and it seemed only sensible then to trust totally in God.... I had talked of trusting him, indeed I truly had trusted him, but never in the sense of abandoning all other sources of support and relying on his grace alone.[18]

In the end, he had learned it, and taught so many others, through word and example, to do the same. Father Ciszek had defended the faith very well indeed.

[18] Ciszek, *He Leadeth Me*, 78.

XVI

A Modern Intellectual Defense
of the Faith:
Joseph Cardinal Ratzinger

Few men in the modern world have given such convincing intellectual defense of the faith as the current Prefect of the Congregation for the Doctrine of the Faith, Joseph Cardinal Ratzinger. It is one of the many proofs of the greatness of Pope John Paul II that he would choose a man of such towering intellect and orthodoxy to fill such a demanding, yet delicate position.

Cardinal Ratzinger was born in April 1927 into a family of moderate financial means in Upper Bavaria. From his father (a constable) and mother he received a deep, abiding Catholic faith. Attendance at Mass and daily prayers in common were merely taken for granted, and interestingly, as a young man he developed a fascination with the Latin language; his parents once gave him a missal, and the youngster became engrossed in translation.

Nationalism did not figure as prominently in the Ratzinger home as religion, but it nonetheless occupied a very prominent role, making it ironic when fifteen-year-old Joseph and his brother were forced to join the Hitler youth movement.

They attended one session and never returned. The irony is to be found in Cardinal Ratzinger's own description of his nationalistic upbringing:

> We were very patriotic Bavarians already by family tradition. Our father came from lower Bavaria, and . . . in the Bavarian politics of the nineteenth century there were two currents. There was one more oriented to the *Reich*, more German nationalistic. The other was a more Bavarian-Austrian . . . Francophile [and] Catholic leaning. My family belonged very clearly to this second current, which was very consciously and patriotically Bavarian and proud of our history. My mother came from Tyrol, but there too . . . this southern German-Catholic element was very strong.[1]

Bavarian Catholicism fostered priestly vocations. Cardinal Fulhauber, Archbishop of Munich, once visited young Joseph Ratzinger's village, greatly impressing the young Ratzinger. This same cardinal would ordain him to the priesthood in 1951. The precise moment, though, when his priestly vocation became a reality was never clear:

> [T]here was no lightning-like moment of illumination when I realized I was meant to become a priest. On the contrary, there was a long process of maturation, and the decision had to be thought through and constantly rewon. I couldn't date the decision, either. But the feeling that God had a plan for each person, for me too, became clear for me early on. Gradually it became clear to me that what he had in mind had to do with the priesthood.[2]

---

[1] Joseph Cardinal Ratzinger, *Salt of the Earth: The Church at the End of the Millennium* (San Francisco: Ignatius Press, 1997), 50.

[2] Ibid., 54.

Neither his minor seminary years nor those of theology were to be uneventful. As a boy of sixteen at the seminary in Traunstein, he and his classmates were as eligible for the wartime draft as other young men their age. They were put into antiaircraft work in Munich and later moved to the Austro-Hungarian border just a short time after Hungary had surrendered to Russia. One year of work on embankments and tank traps allowed him to return to Traunstein, though for a brief time he was incarcerated with fifty thousand inmates in an American prisoner-of-war camp. His years of theological study in Munich involved more of an inner struggle. Natural student that he was, he became fascinated with academics; theology itself greatly absorbed him, since by its very nature it is defined as *fides quaerens intellectum*, "faith seeking understanding". He began to probe its most profound questions and looked forward to a life of study; but the priesthood involves far more. Life in a parish often places demands on men, not allowing much time for scholarly work. Joseph Ratzinger realized that if he were to accept the priesthood, he must embrace it in its entirety.

Reflecting on this years later, Cardinal Ratzinger offers yet another insight:

> When I look back on the exciting years of my theological studies, I can only be amazed at everything that is affirmed nowadays concerning the "preconciliar" Church. All of us lived with a feeling of radical change that had already arisen in the 1920s, the sense of a theology that had the courage to ask new questions and a spirituality that was doing away with what was dusty and obsolete and leading to a new joy in the redemption. Dogma was conceived, not as an external shackle, but as the living source that made knowledge of the truth possible in the first place. The Church came to life for us above all in the liturgy and in the great richness of the theo-

logical tradition. We did not take the demands of celibacy lightly, but we were convinced that we did well to trust the Church's experience of many centuries and that the deep-reaching renunciation she required of us would bear fruit.[3]

Joseph Ratzinger would have his pastoral experience, but his future as a theologian would be ensured during these student years. He and his classmates, all theological students in Munich, were free to enter a yearly contest involving the preparation of a written assignment developed over a nine-month period. Students did not sign their name to these papers; they merely inserted a code. Each year a different professor took charge of the contest and submitted his own topic, ensuring that all areas of theology would be covered. Joseph Ratzinger was a participant in 1950 when the topic was *The People and the House of God in Augustine's Doctrine of the Church*. He had done extensive reading on the Fathers of the Church and had attended one seminar on Augustine, so he felt confident entering the contest. The winner would be provided a small monetary prize, but far more important, the winner's assignment would be given the equivalency of a *summa cum laude* dissertation. Ratzinger won, ensuring future studies.

His reading of the Fathers of the Church took on greater significance when he was introduced to the theology of French Jesuit Henri de Lubac, whose writing enhanced Ratzinger's whole view of theology and faith. De Lubac tried to move from a strictly individualistic view of faith to a more social one, in which one person's faith was part of "our" faith, a faith that affected history as a whole, not merely individuals.

[3] Joseph Cardinal Ratzinger, *Milestones: Memoirs 1929–1977* (San Francisco: Ignatius Press, 1998), 57–58.

Ratzinger became so enamored of de Lubac's thought that he sought out more of his writings; he was especially moved by *Corpus Mysticum*, a work providing him a view of the Eucharist that influenced his future writing.

All of this remained in the future. After Father Ratzinger was ordained to the priesthood on the feast of Ss. Peter and Paul, June 29, 1951, in the Cathedral of Munich, he was assigned as curate at the Church of the Most Precious Blood in one of the city's residential districts. It was a parish of contrasts—there were intellectuals, artists, and Munich's prominent business community, as well as small shopkeepers and those who worked in Munich's wealthy homes. As a priest, Father Ratzinger learned the deep hungers of the human heart.

> In us they saw persons who had been touched by Christ's mission and had been empowered to bring his nearness to men. Precisely because we ourselves were not the point, a friendly human relationship could develop very quickly.[4]

Following his parochial duties, Father Ratzinger was appointed to teach at the seminary at Freisling. He quickly began working on what is known in Germany as the Habilitation degree. Once achieved, an individual is eligible to be considered for a faculty position at a German university. One had to propose a specific thesis and defend it convincingly. Ratzinger chose Saint Bonaventure and his view of revelation. The topic was timely; in the fifties several theologians were placing a new emphasis on revelation, viewing it less as a communication of truths to the mind and more as God's personal action of revealing himself to man. This being the case, the young priest-professor began to investigate what, if

[4] Ibid., 100.

anything, Saint Bonaventure wrote on salvation history concerning the saint's understanding of revelation.

Father Ratzinger's findings initially impacted negatively on him, but in the long run were to be beneficial. His thesis maintained that nothing of our understanding of revelation could be found in Bonaventure's writings. The saintly Franciscan had written in the Middle Ages, when the sole idea of revelation was divine communication. Medieval thought stressed the act of revelation, not the result of the act; the receiving subject to whom revelation is given was not an important component. When there is no receiving subject, there is no revelation; God has not "unveiled" himself to anyone. Such findings were rather novel, leading one examiner to reject Father Ratzinger's thesis on the grounds he had not been faithful to Saint Bonaventure's thought. He did finally earn the Habilitation degree, but not without a stormy defense and a difficult time from his examining board. Regarding the subject of his Habilitation, he later wrote:

> These insights, gained through my reading of Bonaventure, were later on very important for me at the time of the conciliar discussion on revelation, Scripture, and tradition. Because, if Bonaventure is right, then revelation precedes Scripture and becomes deposited in Scripture but is not simply identical with it. This in turn means that revelation is always something greater than what is merely written down. And this again means that there can be no such thing as a pure *sola scriptura* ("by Scripture alone"), because an essential element of Scripture is the Church as understanding subject, and with this the fundamental sense of tradition is already given.[5]

---

[5] Ibid., 108–9.

Joseph Ratzinger would go on to hold distinguished chairs at Bonn, Münster, Tübingen, and Regensburg. In 1977 he was appointed Archbishop of Munich and Freising, but this was not a position he accepted with great initial enthusiasm. He accepted only after much personal prayer and personal consultation with his confessor. Once his appointment became public, he chose as his episcopal motto "Co-worker of the Truth". Since he had formerly been a university professor and was to become a pastoral teacher, he felt the motto expressed the unity between the two. For a thousand years, the coat of arms of the bishops of Freising had displayed a crowned moor. Ratzinger took this to symbolize the unity of the body of Christ, which knows no class distinction. He then selected two additional symbols. The first was a shell, depicting our pilgrim journey through this world; it was also reminiscent of a story concerning Saint Augustine. While walking along the seashore, the saint discovered a young boy trying to pour the entire ocean into the shell. Saint Augustine told the boy that it was no more possible for him to empty the ocean into that shell than it was for the human mind to understand the mystery of God. For Ratzinger, the shell symbolized the profound mystery of God, while also connecting him with his old mentor, Saint Augustine.

The second symbol was a bear, taken from the coat of arms of Corbinian, first Bishop of Freising. The legend is that the bear attacked the Bishop's horse, tearing the animal apart. The Bishop severely reprimanded the bear for this, then took a large pack off the horse and placed it on the bear. The Bishop was traveling to Rome, making the bear carry the burden until they arrived in the Eternal City. The bear's burden was reminiscent of a meditation written by Saint Augustine on the burdens all bishops face. It was based on the Saint's reading of verses 22 and 23 in Psalm 73 (72).

Augustine noted that a bishop often accepts the burden of public disapproval when he teaches what Christ taught, which frequently runs contrary to public opinion. This teaching the new Archbishop of Munich and Freising would proclaim forcefully for four years, until 1981. By now a cardinal (as of June 27, 1977), he was summoned to Rome to be of further service to God and his Church as Prefect of the Sacred Congregation for the Doctrine of the Faith.

In 1978, Cardinal Ratzinger had not the slightest inkling when he made the acquaintance of Poland's Karol Cardinal Wojtyla at the consistory that elected the latter Pope, that he, Ratzinger, would subsequently be named Prefect. In fact, the two men quickly became friends, and the German theologian observed many things about the Pope from Poland:

> The first thing that won my sympathy was his uncomplicated, human frankness and openness, as well as the cordiality that he radiated. There was his humor. You also sensed a piety that had nothing false, nothing external about it. You sensed that here was a man of God. . . . You notice . . . he has suffered, he has also struggled on his way to this vocation. He lived through the whole drama of the German occupation, of the Russian occupation, and of the Communist regime. He blazed his own intellectual trail. . . . He entered deeply into the whole intellectual history of Europe. . . . This intellectual wealth, as well as his enjoyment of dialogue and exchange, these were all things that immediately made him likeable to me.[6]

The Congregation for the Doctrine of the Faith had its origin in the Inquisition. The Cardinal did not, however, think

---

[6] Ratzinger, *Salt of the Earth*, 85.

himself an Inquisitor. Rather, having the belief that only scholarly argument and the appeal to faith are at the basis of the Congregation's existence, he viewed his role as one of service to the Church and of dialogue with theologians and the world's bishops, and they, in turn, with their religious superiors, priests, and all those whose lives brought them in contact with the Congregation's work. He never sought power and did not choose to exercise it in any intimidating way.

The Cardinal Prefect came to world attention four years after assuming his position. In 1985, to commemorate the twentieth anniversary of the closing of the Second Vatican Council, he granted an exclusive interview on the state of the Church to Italian journalist Vittorio Messori. This interview has come to be known in English as *The Ratzinger Report*. It concerned itself with many of the difficulties in the Church, especially the fundamental misunderstanding of the Second Vatican Council's intent. The Council Fathers had worked for a new Catholic unity; instead, what the Cardinal terms a self-criticism entered the ecclesial body, which ultimately became self-destructive. What was intended, he said, was a new enthusiasm; what occurred was a "boredom" and "discouragement". Before the Council's authentic renewal could be a reality, many would have to turn away from the erroneous paths they had followed. One thing was certain: the fault did not lie with the Second Vatican Council:

> I am convinced that the damage that we have incurred in these twenty years is due, not to the "true" Council, but to the unleashing *within* the Church of latent polemical and centrifugal forces; and *outside* the Church it is due to the confrontation with a cultural revolution in the West: the success

of the upper middle class, the new "tertiary bourgeoisie", with its liberal-radical ideology of individualistic, rationalistic and hedonistic stamp.[7]

At the heart of the crisis in the post-conciliar Church, the Cardinal said, was a misunderstanding of the very term "Church". It is the *communio sanctorum*, the Communion of Saints, which includes not only the close intimacy between the Church triumphant, suffering and militant, but also a sharing in her riches, her sacramental life. The efficacy of these sacraments, in which all fully incorporated members living in the state of sanctifying grace share fully, comes to us from the crucified and resurrected Christ. This being the case, Cardinal Ratzinger strongly emphasizes it is Christ's Church, not ours. The only things about the Church we may claim as ours are the external particulars at a given moment in history. If it were only our Church, the Prefect noted, it would be impossible to think of a hierarchical system established by Christ himself, existing solely for service to the faithful:

> It is a rejection of the concept of an authority willed by God, an authority therefore that has its legitimation in God and not . . . in the consensus of the majority of the members of an organization. . . . The Church of Christ is not a party, not an association, not a club. Her deep and permanent structure is not *democratic* but *sacramental*, consequently *hierarchical*. For the hierarchy based on the apostolic succession is the indispensable condition to arrive at the strength, the reality of the sacrament. Here authority is not based on the majority of votes; it is based on the authority of Christ himself,

[7] Joseph Cardinal Ratzinger with Vittorio Messori, *The Ratzinger Report, An Exclusive Interview on the State of the Church* (San Francisco: Ignatius Press, 1985), 30.

which he willed to pass on to men who were to be his rep-
resentatives until his definitive return.[8]

From this misconceived notion of "our" Church, much followed: theologians felt themselves free to market individual
theologies as well as Christologies that depicted Christ in
ways far removed from the Church's understanding of her
Lord. In addition, it led to a separation between Scripture
and Magisterium, particularly as Scripture began to be treated
as a document to be investigated. Finally, the explaining away
of our sinful human condition since the fall could clearly be
seen as a source of the sexual revolution the world came to
know by the 1980s. These and the many other topics the
Cardinal discussed in *The Ratzinger Report* placed him firmly
in one camp: defense of the faith. At the same time, it won
him countless admirers around the world—and not a few
detractors.

Some fifteen years after *The Ratzinger Report*, the Cardinal
granted an interview to Peter Seewald in which he concentrated on the Church at the end of the millennium. The
interview is significant for the candor with which he so clearly
analyzes current trends of thought. One such area is liberation theology, which, in its political emphasis, is too one-
sided. If the Church were aligned with it, she would become
only an advocate for world peace, a geopolitical restructur-
ing of the world, and the preservation of the earth. Further,
when liberation is connected with feminism, women are immediately seen as victims of oppression. When this occurs,
the Cardinal notes, political liberation theology has been replaced by anthropological liberation, one that centers solely
on oppressed human beings, in this case, women. The lib-

[8] Ibid., 49.

eration that seeks to free women from such a status is seen clearly in the sexual revolution:

> The idea that "nature" has something to say is no longer admissible; man is to have the liberty to remodel himself at will. He is to be free from all of the prior givens of his essence. He makes of himself what he wants, and only in this way is he really "free" and liberated.... In the end, it is a revolt against our creatureliness. Man is to be his own creator—a modern, new edition of the immemorial attempt to be God, to be like God.[9]

The trend is not unrelated to feminism; the concepts of mother earth, the feminine in God, and the view that God as Father has traditionally kept women oppressed—are all in some fashion related. Finally, Cardinal Ratzinger sees two other trends "making the circle of the globe": an ecology that has made the cosmos divine, and a form of relativism that holds that any truly democratic view of the world cannot admit that any particular religion possessed the whole truth while others possess only fragments of it. Such a worldview smacks of intolerance and "has made the question of whether we are entitled to go on with our Christian self-understanding a burning one".[10]

Each of these positions has to be met by the Church and engaged in dialogue. Cardinal Ratzinger would never retreat from a situation, nor would he respond in such a way as to alienate secular culture. Rather, he would use his towering intellect to respond, and he would be just as quick to add that intellectual life is nothing if spirituality is lacking. How

---

[9] Ratzinger, *Salt of the Earth*, 133.
[10] Ibid., 134.

then is genuine reform to come to the Church of the third millennium?

> Just think of Benedict, who, at the end of antiquity, created the form of life thanks to which the Church went through the great migrations. Or . . . think of Francis and Dominic—in a feudalistic, ossifying Church, an evangelical movement that lived the poverty of the gospel, its simplicity, its joy. . . The Council of Trent was important, but it could be effective as a Catholic reform only because there were saints like Teresa of Avila, John of the Cross, Ignatius of Loyola, Charles Borromeo, and many others who were simply struck inwardly by the faith, who lived it with originality in their own way, created forms of it, which then made possible necessary, healing reforms. For this reason I would also say that in our time the reforms will definitely not come from forums and synods, though these have their legitimacy, sometimes even their necessity. Reforms will come from convincing personalities whom we may call saints.[11]

Is Joseph Cardinal Ratzinger in his own way one of those saints? Who can say. Certainly he is a convincing personality, a man sent to the Church in our day for her strength, her intellectual vitality, and, most importantly, for the defense of her faith.

---

[11] Ibid., 269–70.

A FINAL WORD

Throughout her two-thousand-year history, Holy Mother Church has had many defenders of the faith, and these have defended her in a variety of ways. In this work, we have very subjectively chosen the areas of martyrdom, the life of the mind, the persuasion of oratory, the power of the printed word, and spirituality as legitimate areas for meditation, and presented personalities whose contributions easily fit such categories. They have much to say to us in an age when the faith is weak, catechesis is poor, lack of knowledge of the truths of Catholicism prevails, and strong personalities, if not heroes, seem to be relegated to near obscurity.

A look at our earliest Christian roots tells us that, if the faith is worth living for, it is also worth dying for. The mere fact that so many have shed their life's blood in defense of a set of truths given us by the Lord himself, allows the heroic to shine forth abundantly. Never was this truer than at the time of the Reformation, when so many, by shedding their blood, demonstrated that they were willing to die for a mystery, but never for a question mark. In the twentieth century, in the face of totalitarian regimes, the life of a Jozsef Mindzenty or a Walter Ciszek sends the same powerful message.

The modern, intellectual and orthodox defense of the faith found in the career of Joseph Cardinal Ratzinger hearkens back to the contributions of Albert, Thomas Aquinas,

Bonaventure, and Augustine. They all remind us to thank God for the wonderful minds of so many solid theologians who have deepened our awareness of the mysteries of God, and also deepened our appreciation for the faith that is in us. Athanasius not only defended the faith intellectually but was willing to go into exile for what he believed.

In an era when new Catholic colleges, universities, and law schools are flourishing because they are committed to the Church's Magisterium and the twenty-first century vision of Pope John Paul II, we need to recall the marvelous contributions of Saint Ignatius of Loyola and the Jesuits whose university system throughout sixteenth-century Europe strengthened the faith in confrontation with the reformers. There was a twentieth-century counterpart in the Catholic intellectual revival of the nineteen twenties and thirties, of which Hilaire Belloc was a wonderful representative, both in his speaking and writing. And, for those who have benefited from so many orthodox writers, publishing houses, and recent Catholic publications—newspapers, magazines, and scholarly journals—it is well to remember the concept is not new; decades ago in the British Isles, the Catholic Truth Society began printing inexpensive materials explaining the faith in a nation that had suffered a religiously troubled past.

Finally, in our time, when seminaries are so much in need of reform, the clergy hungry for an increase in holiness, the laity so poorly instructed in the rudiments of faith, and the moral climate so far from what it was a few short decades past, who could serve as a better role model than Saint Charles Borromeo, who, in the sixteenth century, went into his enormous Archdiocese of Milan, only to find exactly the same situation. Indeed, some have suggested that the Church's critical need in the twenty-first century is for other Borromeos, who are needed to implement what Father Benedict

Groeschel has termed the reform of renewal. It is hoped that the careful perusal of the lives of those chronicled herein will deepen the Catholic reader's appreciation for the Church's past defenders and heighten our awareness for the need for such defense in our own time.

BIBLIOGRAPHY

Abbot, Walter M., S.J., ed. *The Documents of Vatican II.* New York: Herder and Herder; Association Press; America Press, 1966.

Bamber, Canon J. E. *The Lancaster Martyrs.* London: Catholic Truth Society, undated.

Bassett, Bernard, S.J. *The English Jesuits: From Campion to Martindale.* New York: Herder and Herder, 1968.

Beatrice, Pier Franco. *Introduction to the Fathers of the Church.* Vicenza, Italy: Istituto San Gaetano, 1987.

Belloc, Hilaire. *Characters of the Reformation.* Rockford, Ill.: Tan Books and Publishers, 1992.

———. *Essays of a Catholic.* Rockford, Ill.: Tan Books and Publishers, 1992.

———. *Europe and the Faith.* London: Constable and Company, 1924.

Bence-Jones, Mark. *The Catholic Families.* London: Constable and Company, 1992.

Caraman, Philip, S.J. *Saint Philip Howard.* London: Catholic Truth Society, 1985.

Carroll, Warren H. *A History of Christendom* 3 vols. Front Royal, Va.: Christendom College Press, 1985–1993.

Catechism of the Catholic Church. Vatican City: Libreria Editrice Vaticana, 1997.

Chesterton, Gilbert Keith. *Saint Thomas Aquinas.* San Francisco: Ignatius Press, 2002.

———. *The Everlasting Man.* San Francisco: Ignatius Press, 1993.

Ciszek, Walter J., S.J., with Daniel Flaherty, S.J. *He Leadeth Me*. San Francisco: Ignatius Press, 1995.

———. *With God in Russia*. San Francisco: Ignatius Press, 1997.

Cobbett, William. *A History of the Protestant Reformation in England and Ireland*. Rockford, Ill.: Tan Books and Publishers, 1988.

Comby, Jean. *How to Read Church History*. Vol. 1: *From the Beginnings to the Fifteenth Century*. New York: Crossroad, 1992.

———, and Diarmaid MacCulloch. *How to Read Church History:* Vol. 2: *From the Reformation to the Present Day*. New York: Crossroad, 1991.

Delaney, John J. *Dictionary of American Catholic Biography*. Garden City, N.Y.: Doubleday and Company, 1984.

de Lisle, Leanda, and Peter Stanford. *The Catholics and Their Houses*. London: HarperCollins, 1995.

Durant, Will. *The Story of Civilization: Caesar and Christ*. Vol. 3. New York: Simon and Schuster, 1944.

Fisher, John. *Exposition of the Seven Penitential Psalms*. San Francisco: Ignatius Press, 1998.

Foster, Stewart, O.S.M. *Cardinal William Allen: 1532–1594*. London: Catholic Truth Society, 1992.

Giussano, John Peter. *The Life of Saint Charles Borromeo: Cardinal Archbishop of Milan*. 2 vols. London: Burns and Oates, 1884.

Guiney, Louise Imogen. *Blessed Edmund Campion*. London: R. and T. Washbourne, 1914.

Hollis, Christopher. *The Jesuits: A History*. New York: MacMillan Company, 1968.

Hughes, Philip. *A History of the Church*. 3 vols. New York: Sheed and Ward, 1947–1949; rev. ed. 1979.

Ignatius of Loyola. *Spiritual Exercises*. Louis J. Puhl, S.J., trans. Chicago: Loyola University Press, 1951.

Jebb, Reginald and Eleanor. *Testimony to Hilaire Belloc.* London: Methuen and Company, 1956.

Johnson, Timothy. *Bonaventure: Mystic of God's Word.* Hyde Park, N.Y.: New York City Press, 1999.

Knox, Ronald. *Captive Flames.* London: Burns and Oates, 1940.

Lacouture, Jean. *Jesuits: A Multibiography.* Washington, D.C.: Counterpoint, 1995.

Marius, Richard. *Thomas More.* London: Weidenfeld and Nicholson, 1993.

Mindszenty, Jozsef Cardinal. *Memoirs.* New York: MacMillan Publishing, 1974.

Monro, Margaret T., *Blessed Margaret Clitherow.* London: Burns, Oates and Washbourne, 1948.

Monti, James. *The King's Good Servant but God's First: The Life and Writings of St. Thomas More.* San Francisco: Ignatius Press, 1997.

More, Margaret. *The Household of Sir Thomas More.* 6th ed. London: Burns and Oates, 1887.

Morris, Elizabeth. *The Life and Death of Margaret Clitherow.* London: Catholic Truth Society, 1992.

Morris, Kevin L. *Hilaire Belloc: A Catholic Prophet.* London: Catholic Truth Society, 1995.

Nichols, Aidan, O.P. *The Theology of Joseph Ratzinger.* Edinburgh: T. and T. Clark, 1988.

Norman, Edward. *Roman Catholicism in England: From the Elizabethan Settlement to the Second Vatican Council.* Oxford: Oxford University Press, 1986.

Olin, John C. *The Catholic Reformation: Savonarola to Ignatius Loyola.* New York: Harper and Row, 1969.

O'Malley, John W. *The First Jesuits.* Cambridge: Harvard University Press, 1993.

Palmer, R. R., and Joel Colton. *A History of the Modern World.* New York: Alfred A. Knopf, 1965.

Pollen, John Hungerford, S.J., and William McMahon, S.J., eds. *The Venerable Philip Howard, Earl of Arundel.* Vol. 21. London: Catholic Record Society, 1917.

Ralls, Christopher. *The Catholic Truth Society: A New History.* London: Catholic Truth Society, 1993.

Ratzinger, Joseph Cardinal. *Called to Communion: Understanding the Church Today.* San Francisco: Ignatius Press, 1996.

_____. *Milestones: Memoirs 1927–1977.* San Francisco: Ignatius Press, 1998.

_____. *Salt of the Earth: The Church at the End of the Millennium.* San Francisco: Ignatius Press, 1997.

_____, with Vittorio Messori. *The Ratzinger Report.* San Francisco: Ignatius Press, 1985.

Reynolds, E. E. *Saint John Fisher.* New York: P. J. Kenedy and Sons, 1955; rev. ed. Wheathampstead, Hertfordshire: Anthony Clarke Books, 1955, 1972.

Robinson, John Martin. *Arundel Castle.* Chichester: Phillimore and Company, 1994.

_____. The Dukes of Norfolk: A Quincentennial History. Oxford: Oxford University Press, 1982.

Rotelle, John E., O.S.A., ed. *The Life of Saint Augustine by Possidius, Bishop of Calama.* Villanova, Pa.: Augustinian Press, 1988.

Schreck, Alan. *The Compact History of the Catholic Church.* Ann Arbor, Mich.: Servant Books, 1987.

Sheed, Frank J. *The Church and I.* Garden City, N.Y.: Doubleday and Company, 1974.

_____, and Maisie Ward. *Catholic Evidence Training Outlines.* Ann Arbor, Mich.: Catholic Evidence Guild, 1992.

Sheen, Fulton, J. *Treasure in Clay: The Autobiography of Fulton*

J. Sheen. Garden City, N.Y.: Doubleday and Company, 1980; reprinted San Francisco: Ignatius Press, 1993.

Sheridan, Robert E., M.M. *Bishop James F. Walsh As I Knew Him*. Ossining, N.Y.: Maryknoll Publications, 1981.

_____. *Compassion: A Vocational Autobiography with Background of Bishop Francis X. Ford, M.M.* Ossining, N.Y.: Maryknoll Publications, 1982.

Speaight, Robert. *The Life of Hilaire Belloc*. London: Hollis and Carter, 1957.

Stack, George, ed. *Westminster Cathedral: 1985–1995*. London: Westminster Cathedral, 1995.

Thurston, Herbert, S.J., and Donald Attwater, eds., *Butler's Lives of the Saints*. 4 vols. Westminster, Md.: Christian Classics, 1970, 1981, 1987.

Tigar, Clement, S.J. *Forty Martyrs of England and Wales*. London: Office of the Vice-Postulation, 1970.

Tugwell, Simon, O.P., ed. *Albert and Thomas: Selected Writings*. New York: Paulist Press, 1988.

van Bavel, Tarcisius, O.S.A. *Augustine*. Strasbourg: Éditions du Signe, 1996.

Walsh, James, S.J. *Forty Martyrs of England and Wales*. London: Catholic Truth Society, 1997.

Walsh, James E., M.M. *Description of a Missioner*. Ossining, N.Y.: Maryknoll Publications, 1976.

Ward, Maisie. *Unfinished Business*. London: Sheed and Ward, 1964.

Watkin, E. I. *Roman Catholicism in England From the Reformation to 1950*. London: Oxford University Press, 1957.

Waugh, Evelyn. *Edmund Campion*. Oxford: Oxford University Press, 1980.

Waugh, Margaret. *Blessed Philip Howard, Courtier and Martyr*. London: Office of the Vice-Postulation, 1961.

ACKNOWLEDGMENTS

The author and publisher express their appreciation for permissions to the following publishers and copyright holders for permission to reprint excerpts from the following:

Anthony Clarke Books for excerpts from *Saint John Fisher*, by E. E. Reynolds (Wheathampstead, Hertfordshire, England, 1955).

Anthony Jones for excerpts from *Testimony to Hilaire Belloc*, Reginald and Eleanor Jebb (London: Methuen and Company, Ltd., 1956).

Catholic Truth Society, 40–46 Harleyford Road, Vauxhall, London SE11 5AY, www.cts-online.org.uk, for the following works: *Cardinal William Allen: 1532–1594*, by Stewart Foster, O.S.M. (1992); *Saint Philip Howard*, by Philip Caraman, S.J. (1985); *Forty Martyrs of England and Wales*, by Clement Tigar, S.J. (1961); *Forty Martyrs of England and Wales*, by James Walsh, S.J. (1997); *The Life and Death of Margaret Clitherow*, by Elizabeth Morris (1992); *Hilaire Belloc: A Catholic Prophet*, by Kevin L. Morris (1995); *The Lancaster Martyrs* by Canon J. E. Bamber (n.d.) *The Catholic Truth Society: A New History*, by Christopher Ralls (1993).

The Crossroad Publishing Company, New York, and Continuum, London, for *How to Read Church History*, by Jean Comby, vol. 1 (1992) and vol. 2 (1991); Sheed and Ward.

Reprinted by permission of the Continuum International Publishing Group, Ltd., London and New York.

Doubleday (Random House) for *Treasure in Clay*, by Fulton J. Sheen (New York: 1980; reprinted: San Francisco: Ignatius Press, 1993).

The Estate of Evelyn Waugh for excerpts reproduced from *Edmund Campion*, by Evelyn Waugh (copyright © The Master of Campion Hall, 1935; reprinted by Oxford University Press, 1980). Reprinted by permission of PFD on behalf of the Master of Campion Hall, Oxford.

Fordham University Press for *The Catholic Reformation: Savonarola to Ignatius Loyola*, by John C. Olin (New York: Harper and Row, 1969).

Maryknoll Mission Archives, The Maryknoll Fathers and Brothers, Maryknoll, New York, for their kind permission to use excerpts from the following Maryknoll publications: *Bishop James E. Walsh As I Knew Him*, by Robert E. Sheridan (Ossining, New York, 1981); *Compassion: A Vocational Autobiography with Background of Bishop Francis X. Ford*, by Robert E. Sheridan (Ossining, New York, 1982); and *Description of a Missioner* by James E. Walsh (Ossining, New York, 1976).

Orion Publishing Group, Ltd., for permission to reprint excerpts from *Memoirs*, by Jozsef Cardinal Mindszenty (New York: Macmillan Publishing, 1974). Used with permission of the Orion Publishing Group, Ltd., London.

Paulist Press, for excerpts from *Albert and Thomas: Selected Writings*, by Simon Tugwell, O.P. (New York, © 1988). Used with permission of Paulist Press, www.paulistpress.com.

Peters Fraser and Dunlop Group, Ltd. (PFD), for permission to reprint excerpts from *Testimony to Hilaire Belloc*. Reprinted by permission of PFD on behalf of Reginald and Eleanor Jebb, © 1979, Reginald and Eleanor Jebb.

Rowman and Littlefield Publishing Group, Maryland, for *Unfinished Business*, by Maisie Ward (London, Sheed and Ward, 1964).

Sheed and Ward, London, for *History of the Church*, by Philip Hughes (1935, 1949).

Simon and Schuster for permission to reprint, in the United States, Canada and the Philippines, excerpts from Jozsef Cardinal Mindzenty's *Memoirs*, translated by Richard and Clara Winston. (New York: MacMillan, 1974). Reprinted with the permission of Scribner, an imprint of Simon and Schuster Adult Publishing Group. English translation copyright © 1974 by Macmillan Publishing Company, Inc.

Thomas More Publishing and Continuum Books, London and New York, for *Butler's Lives of the Saints*, ed. Herbert J. Thurston, S.J., and Donald Attwater (Westminster, Md.: Christian Classics, 1987).

Thomas N. O'Brien for *Catholic Evidence Guild Training Outlines*, by Frank Sheed and Massie Ward (London, Catholic Evidence Guild, 1992).

Weidenfeld and Nicolson, Ltd., for world rights to reprint excerpts from Jozsef Cardinal Mindzenty's *Memoirs* (New York: MacMillan Publishing, 1974).

Weidenfeld and Nicolson, Ltd., for Richard Marius, *Thomas More* (London, 1993). All attempts at tracing the copyright holder of this book were unsuccessful.

Wilfred Sheed for Frank Sheed, *The Church and I* (Garden City, N.Y.: Doubleday, 1974).